Piccolo

Games f

Piccolo Book of Games for Journeys

Deborah Manley and Peta Rée

Cover illustration by Malcolm English
Text illustrations by R. Fishwick

A Piccolo Original

Pan Books Ltd : London

First published 1972 by Pan Books Ltd,
33 Tothill Street, London, SW1.

ISBN 0 330 23215 0

2nd Printing 1972

To Roy and Harry who drove us
and to Carey, Georgia, Brett
and Adam with whom we have driven
many miles

Made and printed in Great Britain by
Hunt Barnard Printing Ltd., Aylesbury, Bucks.

Contents

Introduction

'Long journeys are very boring, aren't they?' said Adam, looking crossly out of the car window, and kicking the back of his father's driving seat.

'Don't do that,' said his father irritably for the third time. 'If you do it again I'll stop the car and heave you out, and you can walk home!'

'Why don't you play some game?' suggested Mother.

'What games can you play in a car?' asked Mark.

'I know one,' said Harriet.

'So do I,' said Catherine.

And these are some of the games they played. And you can play them, too, on journeys in trains and cars.

Chapter One
Before You Start

It is a good idea to make some preparations before the journey begins.

There are some things it is useful to have always in the car, such as:

paper handkerchiefs;
Biro pen or pencil and pencil sharpener;
a small pad of paper;
I-Spy books (more about these later);
a map of the area;
a tin of boiled sweets (barley sugar is best).

For longer journeys we suggest you might add some or all of the following:

- a damp flannel or sponge in a plastic bag (even nicer for warm sticky faces and hands if a few drops of lavender water or eau de cologne are added);
- enough pencils or pens for everyone;
- plenty of paper;
- guide books of the area;
- a rug;
- a pillow (either a full-sized one, or a smaller head pillow, about one foot square) for each child;
- plastic bags for damp swimming things, rubbish, etc, and for collecting such things as stones, shells, plants, bones, fish, bottle tops;
- counters or beans or buttons in a container with a lid.

If you have a car radio, it's worth looking at *The Radio Times* before you leave, because there may be programmes you would like to hear, and would otherwise miss.

Chapter Two
Playing with Words

Sausages: one player is chosen as the victim. All the others ask him all sorts of personal questions to which he may only reply 'sausages'. The aim of the game is to make the victim smile or laugh, and when he does someone takes his place. The questions should be such as to make the answer as extraordinary as possible. You could use a different answering word, such as hippopotamus or gym-shoes.

The conversation might go like this:

What do you clean your teeth with?
Sausages.
What do you love best?
Sausages.
What are you wearing to the party on Saturday?
Sausages.

Last Letter Chain: the first player says the name of a country, town, person, animal, plant, or whatever group of things you have decided to use. The next person has to say another name of the same kind which starts with the last letter of the previous word. The game can last until either someone breaks the chain, or all but one have broken it, leaving that one the winner. Or, to make the game last longer, you may have three 'lives' to lose before you are finally out.

Examples:

German*y*, *Y*ugoslavi*a*, *A*ustria . . .

Londo*n*, *N*ew Yor*k*, *K*ettering . . .
Ca*t*, *t*ige*r*, *r*accoon . . .

Last Word Chain: this game is played like the last one, except that the first player says a phrase, or group of words that 'belong' together. The next person starts his phrase with the last word of the preceding phrase. The game might go like this:

Mark: Four and twenty blackbirds.
Catherine: Birds of a feather.
Adam: Feather bed.
Harriet: Bed time.
Mark: Time for tea.
Catherine: Tea for two.
Adam: Two a penny.
Harriet: Penny for your thoughts.

Spelling Games
These games can be played in teams or between individuals.

Spelling Bee: players take it in turns to spell words given by the question master – who should know how to spell them himself!

Backward Spelling Bee: as above, but spelling the words backwards.

Spelling in Turns: the question master gives a word, and the players take it in turn to provide the next letter. If you give a wrong letter, you drop out of the game, and the next person has to give the right one.
Example:

Catherine: Spell QUEUE
Harriet: Q

Mark: u
Adam: u
Catherine: No, drop out.
Harriet: e
Mark: u
Harriet: e

Making a Word: no word is given here. Players take it in turn to contribute a letter towards a word. Thus, for instance, Adam says 'E', Catherine decides to make the word 'elemental' and says 'l', Mark decides to choose 'elephant' and says 'e' and Harriet also thinking of 'elephant' follows with 'p'. Now it is obvious what the word must become, but the player who gives the last letter of the word loses one of his three lives. The skill therefore is in turning a word which is about to finish into something longer; for instance, elephant can go on to end with s, iasis, ine, inely.

Any player who cannot see the way the word is to continue may challenge the previous player to say what he is spelling. If he cannot give the word (because he didn't know what he *was* spelling! or was spelling wrongly) he loses a life, but if he has a real word the challenger loses a life. Once three lives are lost, a player must drop out of the game.

No Vowel Spelling: there are two ways to play this game. The simpler one involves spelling a word given by the question master but missing out the vowels, so that *telegraph* is spelt *tlgrph*. A more complex version is to substitute a gesture for each vowel, thus:

A – raise your left hand
E – raise your right hand
I – shut your eyes
O – open your mouth wide
U – touch your nose

So, if you are spelling *curtain*, it becomes C – touch your nose – RT – raise your left hand – shut your eyes – N. You lose a life if you say a vowel or use a wrong gesture. There is a limit of three lives.

Spelling with Words: the question master points to a player and says a 3- or 4-letter word; he may spell it out, thus: Dog, D-O-G. He then starts to count, and before he reaches ten, the player must name objects beginning with the letters of the word, thus: Donkey, Orange, Garage.

WHAT LIES AT THE BOTTOM OF THE SEA AND SHIVERS?

A NERVOUS WRECK.

Initials: players take it in turns to call out a group of initials, and the other players have to suggest what they stand for. The one who gives the most suitable or amusing meaning scores a point. The umpire's decision is final! The game can also be played by the challenger having his own meaning, and the others trying to guess it. This is easier in a family, where one knows the sort of thing the others are likely to think of. Examples:

I–L–D = I like driving
A–W–N–T = Are we nearly there?

Numbers: similar to Initials, but here players have to provide a suitable word to match up with a given number. Examples:

1 – old maid
2 – for a wedding
3 – bears
9 – days' wonder
21 – for the key of the door (maybe should be 18 now)
60 – a diamond wedding

What is your Hobby? Each player makes up a hobby

(it can be as ridiculous and unlikely as you please), the first word of which begins with the initial of his first name, and the second word with the initial of his surname. Thus:

What is your hobby? Catching Monkeys says Catherine Murphy
What is your hobby? Hanging Gardens says Harriet Gill

When everyone has had a turn, you could go on to the hobbies of famous people, for instance:

What was Horatio Nelson's hobby? Hatching Newts.
What was Napoleon Bonaparte's hobby? Nibbling Babies.

Pronounce Me: the question master asks the players to pronounce words which he either writes down or spells out, grouping the letters in an unusual way. Examples:

JA-WA-CHES	MAC-HINE-RY	HA-IRN-ET
(Jaw aches)	(Machinery)	(Hairnet)

Pippety-pop: one player points to another of the group and says either 'pippety-pop' or 'poppety-pip'; he tries to say it as unexpectedly as possible. The one pointed to must immediately reply with whichever alternative the first player did not use. If he says the wrong one, he takes over as 'it'. This game should be mixed in with other games or ordinary conversation so it is easier to catch people out!

One Fat Hen: this game works on the 'cumulative list' principle, (but is easier for small children, because there is a repetitive element and there is a leader). The leader begins, and each player repeats the list after him in turn. The leader adds one item to the list in each round – so, with three players, the game could start like this:

Mark: One fat hen
Harriet: One fat hen
Adam: One fat hen
Mark: Two tame turkeys and one fat hen

The leader must use phrases whose words start with the same sound. Here are some suggestions – you can think up others of your own:

Three thousand thrushes
Four fierce foxes
Five feathered friends
Six sick sisters
Seven surly servants
Eight ailing angels
Nine knitting nitwits
Ten tubby tortoises, etc.

WHAT IS GREEN AND HAIRY AND GOES UP AND DOWN?

A GOOSEBERRY IN A LIFT.

Beast, Bird, Fish: one player challenges another, surprising him if he can, by pointing at him and saying (for example) 'Beast, bird, fish, – beast'. The other player tries to name a 'beast', such as 'cat', before the challenger can count to ten. You can also play this game as 'Earth, air, fire, water'. For 'earth' you must say an animal which walks, for 'air' one that flies, for 'water' one that swims; but for 'fire' the answer is complete silence.

Similes (phrases which say that something is like or as something else): the challenger says an uncompleted simile, which is in established use, and the one next to him must complete it; if he does it correctly a point goes to him, if he does it wrongly or if he doesn't know it, the point goes to the challenger. The first to reach five points is the winner. The simile can be given either way round, eg, either:

as happy as . . . or . . . as a sandboy

Associations: players take it in turns to say the first word that comes into their head, each producing a word which has been suggested to them by the last person's word. The game must move quickly, and he who hesitates is lost, until one player is left the winner.

Pot of Gold: one player starts the game by saying, 'If I found a pot of gold I would buy . . .' and then describes an object he would buy, without mentioning its name. The other players try to guess what it is. The first player to guess right becomes the buyer in the next round.

Yes and No: this game can be played over the whole course of a journey or for an agreed time. Each player is given ten beans or counters. During conversation the players have to try to get a 'Yes' or 'No' out of the others and avoid saying these words themselves. When a person answers 'Yes' or 'No' he has to forfeit a bean to the person he said it to. The winner is the one with the most beans at the end of the game.

No Yes, No No: this is a question and answer game. One player answers questions put to him by the others, and must not answer with 'Yes' or 'No'. When he does it is someone else's turn. It is important to keep the questions and answers going quickly; the questioned player must not hesitate or take time to consider his answers. You must forbid people getting round it by saying things like, 'I can't say', 'I don't know', and affirmative or negative grunts naturally count as 'Yes' or 'No'. A game might go like this:

Mark: It's a nice day, isn't it?
Catherine: A bit cloudy.
Harriet: But the sun's shining, isn't it?
Catherine: Not very brightly.
Mark: Do you like the sun?
Catherine: I like sun-bathing.
Adam: Have you done any lately?
Catherine: Yes, last week . . . (out)

Questions: this game can be fairly simple or it can be most complicated. The idea is that two players carry on a conversation using questions only, making no statements. Example:

Adam: What's your name?
Mark: You want to know my name?
A: Are you going to tell me?
M: What will you do if I don't?
A: What do you think I will do?
M: How should I know?
A: Can't you guess?
M: No. (and so he loses)

Here, from Tom Stoppard's play *Rosenkrantz and Guildenstern are Dead* is a very complicated game of Questions. When the play was performed, the audience always loved this bit.

Rosenkrantz: We could play at questions.
Guildenstern: What good would that do?
R: Practice!
G: Statement! One love.
R: Cheating!
G: How?
R: I hadn't started yet.
G: Statement. Two love.
R: Are you counting that?
G: What?

R: Are you counting that?
G: Foul! No repetitions. Three love. First game.
R: I'm not going to play if you're going to be like that.
G: Whose serve?
R: Hah?
G: Foul! No grunts. Love one.
R: Whose go?
G: Why?
R: Why not?
G: What for?
R: Foul! No synonyms! One all.
G: What in God's name is going on?
R: Foul! No rhetoric. Two one.
G: What does it all add up to?
R: Can't you guess?
G: Were you addressing me?
R: Is there anyone else?
G: Who?
R: How would I know?
G: Why do you ask?
R: Are you serious?
G: Was that rhetoric?
R: No.
G: Statement! Two all. Game point.
R: What's the matter with you today?
G: When?
R: What?
G: Are you deaf?
R: Am I dead?
G: Yes or no?
R: Is there a choice?
G: Is there a God?
R: Foul! No *non-sequiturs*, three two, one game all.

It takes practice to play this game as skilfully as Rosenkrantz and Guildenstern did!

Talking Contest: two players are given a subject, and in turn have to talk upon it for 30 seconds without pausing. The others judge them on their ability to keep going, their eloquence and their inventiveness.

Taboo: this is played the same way as the Talking Contest, but to complicate matters there is a taboo on using one common word, eg, then.

Stories from a Box: from various assorted articles in a box or bag provided, draw out two or three and make up a story round them.

The Chain Story: one person starts a story and after a certain time breaks off (probably a half to one minute is ample if it is being spoken; if written, two minutes at least will be needed. Also, if they are being written, there can be as many stories as there are players). Here is an example of the game being played from E. V. Lucas' *The Slowcoach*, which is a story written at the beginning of this century, about a group of children who receive a present of a caravan from an unknown person, and go for a holiday in it. This game took place when they were visiting some student friends at Oxford.

> This is the one begun by Hester who liked to be serious and mysterious in her work, and was almost vexed when others turned it to nonsense. She called it 'The Secret of the Castle', and it began like this:
>
> 'It was a dark and gloomy night in the year 1135, when the young Lord Almeric reached his impressive and ancestral home. Nothing could be heard but the sighing of the wind in the turrets and the moaning of Boris, the great wolfhound. Lord Almeric had ridden far, and was tired, and the gloominess of his ancestral home weighed on his spirits, which were naturally buoyant and high. Flinging himself from his gaily

caparisoned horse, and tossing the reins with a muttered, "Here, varlet!" to the waiting groom, he opened the massive doors and entered the hall. What was his amazement to see —'

'Time!' called the Snarker, who had his watch before him, and Hester had to stop.

Gregory came next. His idea of the game was not very clear, to begin with, and he had some difficulty in reading what was written, so he was able to write very little, and that not too helpfully. He therefore wrote words that were always near his heart:

'— a flying-machine,'

and that was all.

Then came Janet. Always wishing to be kind and make things easy, she longed to get the story back into the spirit and period of poor little romantic Hester's opening passages. But Gregory had spoiled everything. Janet, however, did her best:

'The young lord drew back with a start, for he could hardly believe his eyes. "What," he exclaimed, "is this strange mixture of wires and wings? Can my father's astrologer have really done it at last after all these fruitless years? He must indeed have been busy since I rode forth to battle. Zounds, do I dream or wake?" He touched the strange thing cautiously, but it did not bite, and gradually there came upon him an exceeding desire to fly. "By my halidom," he cried, "I will e'en inquire further into this mystery —".'

Next came Fizzy, who was bent on being funny at any cost. He wrote:

'— as the man said, sticking his fork into the German sausage. "What ho, my merry minions, help!" he cried. "Let us draw forth the areoplane into the home meadow, for I would fain experiment with it. A lord is no lord unless he can daunt the swallow and the pigeon." So saying, he rang the alarm bell, which was kept only for fires and burglaries, and summoned the household. "A murrain on ye for being so pestilent slow!" he shouted. "Gadsooth, ye knaves! let loose the petrol, or I soar not into the zenith." '

Then came Mary, who naturally had no patience with nonsense. She ignored Fizzy's contribution completely, and got back to romance:

'Meanwhile, seated in her room in the home turret sat the lovely Lady Elfrida, the picture of woe. Why did her lord tarry? Had she not heard him ride into the courtyard and give his palfrey to the waiting serf? Yet where was he? He was wont to spring up the stairs lightly as a roebuck of the mountains to welcome her, and now where was he? Little did she guess —'

Here Shrimp took the paper and wrote:

'— that a brand-new monoplane was blocking up the stairs, so big that not a roebuck on earth could jump it. But what of the secret of the castle? Was that the secret? No. Why did the wind shriek and the deerhound moan? If you would know this, reader, come with me down the dungeon steps and unbar yonder dark door. For there in the dark recess of that terrible cell lay —'

The Shrimp, even although time had not been called, was very glad to leave off here. Robert took the paper. He read the narrative as well as he could, and added these words:

'But I cannot bring my pen to write the word. It was a secret; indeed, the secret of the castle. No wonder that the dog moaned and the wind howled and the Lady Elfrida grieved.'

The Snarker, who, after all, had begun the wretched game, and whose duty it was, therefore, to pull this ruin of a story together again, ought to have played fair; but instead he went back to what Fizzy had called an 'areoplane', spelling not being taught at Oxford. He therefore wrote:

'And meanwhile, what of the aeroplane? Fortunately,

the night was short, and there was soon enough light by which to fly, and in a brief time the seneschals and myrmidons had the great machine in the midst of the tourney-ground, all ready for flight. Lord Almeric seated himself and grasped the lever. A firm push from the willing arms of a hundred carles and hinds, and he was in the air. "Ah," he cried, "odds bodkins, this is indeed life! Never have I felt such sensations. I will never walk or ride again. I will sell my motor-car and my horses and my boots. Flying for me for ever!" '

Jack now took the paper:

'Lord Almeric was always a very clever man, and it was nothing to him that he had never flown before. He had studied the pictures of the flying men in the illustrated papers while waiting at the dentist's, and he knew the principles of mechanics. No wonder, then, that he flew with perfect control, circling the home turret where the Lady Elfrida was still weeping, with the greatest ease, and calling to her messages of comfort, which —'

Here the Snarker called 'Time' again, and Mr Lennox's young brother took the paper:

'— she could not hear. "Come down, good lord, or of a verity thou wilt fall and crack thy coxcomb!" shouted the major-domo from beneath; but the intrepid Almeric heeded not the warning, and only rose higher and higher, nearer and nearer to the stars. And then, suddenly, there was an awful shriek, and his body was seen to be hurtling steadily and surely towards the earth, gaining speed with every revolution. "Help, help!" they cried; "he must be dashed to pieces; nothing can save him." But at that moment —'

Here Horace had to go on. He was not a literary boy, and it took him more than one minute to read all that had gone before. All he could therefore add was:

'— he woke up. "Where am I?" he said. "You have fallen out of bed," said Lady Elfrida.'

Poor Hester! her face was a picture of perplexity and indignation when she came to read the story all through. There was clearly no sensible ending possible, and she therefore merely wrote:

'Not to this day has the secret of the Castle been solved, but visitors are still shown, on payment of a shilling each, the place where Lord Almeric dreamed he fell from a flying-machine in the year 1135.'

A MAN WAS ONCE HUNTING FOR ELEPHANTS IN THE JUNGLE. AFTER MANY A WEARY MILE WITHOUT SUCCESS, AT LENGTH HE CAME UPON TWO ELEPHANTS. THEY WERE SITTING BACK TO BACK IN THE MIDDLE OF A CLEARING. THE HUNTER WAS A VERY SPORTING MAN, AND HE DID NOT WISH TO SHOOT A SITTING TARGET, SO HE APPROACHED ONE OF THE ELEPHANTS, TAPPED IT ON THE SHOULDER, AND POLITELY ASKED IT TO GET UP. THE ELEPHANT LOOKED ROUND AT HIM VERY CROSSLY AND SAID 'OH, DO GO AWAY. WE'RE PLAYING AT BEING BOOK-ENDS.'

Chapter Three
From A to Z

Alphabet Collecting: there are various versions of this game. In all of them the players, as they travel along, look out for objects beginning with letters of the alphabet in order. The simplest collection is of any object at all, as: aeroplane, baby, cow, dog, etc.

Another collection could be words on signs or hoardings, as: anti-freeze, bank, caravan site, concealed drive, entrance, etc.

A more difficult collection is one limited by subject, such as a 'Nature' collection, thus: apple tree, bird, cat, daisy, etc. Or an inn-sign collection: the archer, the boar, etc.

Each item may only be used by the first player who sees it. If played competitively, the winner is the one who is furthest through the alphabet at the end of the journey.

Alphabet Sentences: there are three versions of this game, which is not a competition, but contributed to by everyone who can. The simplest version is to choose a word and make a sentence using each letter in order as initial letters in the words of the sentence, thus:

DRIVER
Do rivers in Venice ever rise?

A more complex way to play is to make a sentence in

which every word begins with a different letter of the alphabet, not necessarily in order.

The most difficult version is to make a sentence using all the alphabet in order, so you might begin:

A badly chastened doleful elephant forcefully gave his Indian jemadar ...

You will find you keep getting into cul-de-sacs by using grammatical structures which compel you to use words in a certain order, and you have to back-track and re-start; but it can be done, and at last you can triumphantly announce whatever is your version of the Excited Youthful Zebras. (You are allowed to cheat on X by using words which start with the sound of X.)

HOW CAN YOU TELL IF THERE'S AN ELEPHANT IN THE REFRIGERATOR?

YOU CAN'T SHUT THE DOOR.

Alphabet Games: the next group of games are different forms of the same basic idea; that is, taking turns to complete a set of statements with words starting with the letters of the alphabet in order. You might like to make up similar games of your own.

Who are You?
My name is *Anna*
My husband's name is *Andrew*
We live in *Andover*
And we sell *Apples*

My name is *James*
My wife's name is *Jane*
We live in *Jarrow*
And we sell *Jewels*

I Love my Love
I love my love with an *L* because she is *Lucky*
I hate her with an *L* because she is too *Lively*

Her name is *Lucy*
And I feed her on *Lollypops*

A was an Apple Pie

Here is a version from an old Nursery Rhyme book. The Tragic Death of A, Apple Pie,
Who was cut in pieces, and eaten by twenty-five gentlemen, with whom all little people ought to be very well acquainted.

A was an Apple pie,
B bit it,
C cut it,
D dealt it,
E eat it,
F fought for it,
G got it,
H had it,
I inspected it,
J joined for it,
K kept it,
L longed for it,
M mourned for it,
N nodded at it,
O opened it,
P peeped in it,
Q quartered it,
R ran for it,
S stole it,
T took it,
U upset it,
V viewed it,
W wanted it,
XYZ and all wished for a piece in hand.

You could make up your own version, each player taking it in turn to say what each letter of the alphabet did to some thing.

My Grandmother's Cat: in this game, each person produces a word for each letter, so, with three players, the game might go like this:

Catherine: My grandmother's cat is an atrocious cat.
Harriet: My grandmother's cat is an amiable cat.
Mark: My grandmother's cat is an artful cat.
Catherine: My grandmother's cat is a boring cat ...
and so on.

Where Are You Going?
This version uses question and answer, thus:

Where are you going?
I am going to *Athens*
What will you do there?
Admire the *Acropolis*.
Where are you going?
I am going to *Birmingham*.
What will you do there?
Butter Buns.

HOW CAN YOU TELL THERE'S AN ELEPHANT IN THE REFRIGERATOR?

THE GIRAFFES HAVE ALL BEEN PUSHED OUT ON THE FLOOR.

I Packed my Bag: this is a 'cumulative memory' game. Each player in turn says what he packed in his bag, first listing everything everyone else has put in, and then adding an item of his own. This need not be played alphabetically, but it is much easier when it is. If a player misses out anything he drops out, and the last person who is able to complete the whole list is the winner. A game might start like this:

Adam: I packed my bag and in it I put an anorak.

Mark: I packed my bag and in it I put an anorak and a butter dish.
Harriet: I packed my bag and in it I put an anorak, a butter dish, and a comb.

Chapter Four
Think of a Number

Sum Bee: this is organized like a spelling bee with a question master asking questions of individuals or teams. The questions can be varied so that even the youngest players can take part, answering simple questions such as 'How many eyes have you?' or 'Hold up three fingers.' Questions can range from these very easy ones to 'What is the square root of 144?'

Think of a Number: the leader says to another player 'Think of a number . . . double it . . . add on (a chosen even number) . . . halve it . . . subtract (half the previously mentioned even number) . . . and the answer is the number you first thought of.'

Thus: Think of a number: 8; double it: 16; add on 4: 20; halve it: 10; take away 2; and the answer is 8.

Or a more spectacular version: Think of a number between 1 and 9 . . . multiply it by 3 . . . add 1 . . . multiply by 3 again . . . add on the number first thought of . . . you will now have a number which ends with 3 . . . discard that 3, and you will be left with the number you first thought of.

Thus: Think of a number: 6; multiply it by 3: 18; add 1: 19; multiply it by 3: 57; add on 6: 63; discard the 3; and you are left with 6.

If you want to know why these work, look on page 106.

Bang and Buzz: the idea is to substitute the words 'bang' and 'buzz' respectively, for the multiples of two previously agreed upon numbers between 1 and 9. So, if you have settled that the numbers are to be 3 and 5, the game will go as follows, each person speaking in turn: 1 – 2 – bang – 4 – buzz – bang – 7 – 8 – bang – buzz – 11, and so on, as long as you like. Where both numbers go into the multiple, the speaker must say 'bang and buzz' (as in this case for 15). A player loses a life if he says a figure when he should have said bang or buzz, or if he says bang instead of buzz or buzz instead of bang.

Doubling: a mental arithmetic game which can be played by one person on his own, or by a number of people in turn. You start with a number between 1 and 9 and go on doubling it until you can work it out in your head no farther, thus: 1, 2, 4, 8, 16, 32, 64, 128, and so on.

Find your Number: use this table to find the 'numbers' of your own name.

A = 1 = 1	N = 14 = 5	
B = 2 = 2	O = 15 = 6	
C = 3 = 3	P = 16 = 7	
D = 4 = 4	Q = 17 = 8	
E = 5 = 5	R = 18 = 9	
F = 6 = 6	S = 19 = 1	(10, and 1+0 = 1)
G = 7 = 7	T = 20 = 2	
H = 8 = 8	U = 21 = 3	
I = 9 = 9	V = 22 = 4	
J = 10 = 1	W = 23 = 5	
K = 11 = 2	X = 24 = 6	
L = 12 = 3	Y = 25 = 7	
M = 13 = 4	Z = 26 = 8	

Now, say your name is GEORGIA BRETT, using the first column of figures, add up the numbers for the letters of each of your names, as:

GEORGIA = 7+5+15+18+7+9+1 = 62 and 6+2 = 8

BRETT = 2+18+5+20+20 = 65 and 6+5 = 11 and 1+1 = 2

Now do it again, but using the second column of figures:

GEORGIA = 7+5+6+9+7+9+1 = 44 and 4+4 = 8

BRETT = 2+9+5+2+2 = 20 and 2+0 = 2

You can do this with any name or address.

Tables: take it in turns to say a table, in the following way. The leader tells a player which table it is to be, say the 5 times, and the player goes through the table, not saying 5 times 1 is 5, 5 times 2 is 10, etc, but just saying 5, 10, 15, 20, 25, and so on. If he makes a mistake, he loses one of his three lives, and the next player starts that table again from the beginning. To make it more difficult you can go backwards through a table, as, in the case of 5 times, 60, 55, 50, 45, 40, and so on. The winner is the last one left with a life.

Multiplying Licences: the leader chooses an oncoming car and reads off its licence number. The players have to multiply its numbers together: for instance, 723 = 7×2×3 = 42. If some of the players are quicker than others, the leader can give the numbers out in turn, perhaps choosing easy or difficult ones to suit the particular player.

Number Puzzles and Trick Questions: there are innumerable number puzzles, and you could collect them to use at suitable moments. Here are a few. The answers are on page 106.

1. Cannibals and Missionaries: three missionaries were being guided through the jungle by three cannibals, and by and by they came to a river. There was a canoe drawn up on the bank, but it would carry only two people at a time. The cannibals were very pleased at this, as it was getting near dinner-time, and they decided that the minute there were two of them and only one missionary on either side of the river, they would overpower him and eat him up. However, the chief missionary, divining their intention, was too clever for them, and arranged the ferrying operation so that this situation never arose. How did he do it?

2. **The Rope Ladder:** a rope ladder was hanging over the side of a ship, with its bottom rung just touching the water. If its rungs are nine inches apart, how many will be under the water when the tide has risen 3 feet?

3. **Coal and Feathers:** which weighs more: a ton of coal or a ton of feathers?

4. **What Is the Next Letter?** Find the next letter in these series and then make up series of your own with numbers or letters.

A D A E A F A —
B E I N —
2 4 8 — 32

Chapter Five
Guess What?

How Many? Each player is given six dried peas or beans or counters. They take it in turns to offer a closed hand to the group and challenge them to guess how many beans are in it. If someone guesses correctly, everyone gives him one bean; if nobody guesses right, everyone gives the challenger a bean. The winner is the player with the most beans at the end of an agreed time.

I Spy: one player says 'I spy with my little eye something begining with —', and he gives the letter of the alphabet with which his chosen object begins. The others have to guess what it is, but the spyer must only answer 'Yes' or 'No' to their questions. The thing spied must be able to be seen constantly, so it could be grass, or the steering wheel, or your hand, but could not be a windmill which has passed out of sight. The players can take turns to be spyer, or the next turn may go to the one who guessed correctly.

HOW DO YOU GET AN ELEPHANT DOWN FROM A TREE?

PUT HIM ON A LEAF AND WAIT TILL AUTUMN.

Heads and Tails: you can play spinning a coin and guessing whether it will come up heads or tails; this is more fun if you use the coins themselves as prizes. Have a bag of 24 pennies and let the players take turns to call. If one is right, he takes the coin; if wrong, it is spun for the next player.

Which Card? The leader holds a pack of cards face

down, and turns them over one by one. The players take turns to call whether the next card will be heart, diamond, club or spade. If a player is right he takes the card; if wrong, the card goes to the bottom of the pack. For a short game, the winner is the one with most cards when the pack has been gone through once, but for a longer game, you can continue until all the cards have been taken from the pack. If you're playing with a very young brother or sister, you might only make them guess whether the card will be red or black.

Animal, Vegetable or Mineral: this is also called Twenty Questions. One player thinks of something which falls into one of the categories (you can also include 'Abstract' with older players). He then says, for example, 'I'm thinking of something Animal.' The others try to guess what it is, by asking questions, such as 'Is it a man? 'Has it four legs?' etc. Only questions which can be answered 'Yes' or 'No' are allowed, and only twenty questions in all may be asked. As soon as a questioner thinks he has guessed, he can ask specifically, as 'Is it Daddy?' The players either take turns to be the challenger or win their turn by guessing correctly. If nobody guesses the object, the challenger may have another turn. For greater difficulty, you may have combinations of two or more categories, as:

Animal and Vegetable – a Donkey eating a Carrot;
Mineral and Vegetable – a Spade.

What Do I Look Like? This should not, strictly speaking, be a guessing game, but will probably turn out to be one! The object is to see how well you know what a friend or even your own brother or sister looks like. There are two ways of playing: either all the players except the 'subject' close their eyes, and the subject then asks each a question in turn, or one player closes his eyes and all the others ask him questions about the subject. Some questions which might be asked are: what colour are her eyes, what colour is her dress, is he wearing socks, which of his teeth is missing, has she a hair ribbon?

A Few Riddles and Trick Questions: Here are a few old chestnuts that the authors remember from their own youth. We hope you can add new riddles and tricks of your own to our list. The answers are on page 106.

1. What goes up the chimney down but not down the chimney up?
2. What is black and white and red all over?
3. What has four wheels and flies?
4. What goes 99 bump, 99 bump?
5. Constantinople is a very long word. How do you spell it?
6. Ninny Nanny Netticoat,
   In a white petticoat,
   With a red nose –
   The longer she stands,
   The shorter she grows.
   What is it?
7. What is the difference between Noah's Ark and Joan of Arc?
8. What is the difference between a buffalo and a bison?
9. What is the difference between an elephant and a letter-box?
10. Why did the chicken cross the road?
11. Where was Moses when the light went out?
12. Two legs sitting on three legs when in came four legs. What happened?
13. Adam and Eve and Pinch-Me went down to the river to bathe. If Adam and Eve were drowned who do you think was saved?

14. What is worse than raining cats and dogs?
15. What is worse than a worm in your apple?

Conundrums: a conundrum is a riddle based on a pun. Here are some examples; you can go on to invent your own. Answers are on page 107.

1. What author is eaten for breakfast?
2. What letter is an insect?
3. What letter do we drink?
4. Which tree is still there after it has burnt down?
5. Which T is lovely?
6. When is a door not a door?
7. What flower is sown by Cupid's dart?
8. Which city has very little?
9. Why does a king bring bad weather?
10. What table can be served at table?

Off to Europe: this game can only be played once with any one group, as it depends on only one person being in the know. This person says 'I'm off to Europe and I'm taking . . .' and names some object beginning with the first letter of his own name. The others then have to say what they are off to Europe with, trying to guess why a particular word is 'right' or 'wrong'. When a player guesses the trick, he or she can join in giving a 'right' word. So a game might go like this:

Adam: I'm off to Europe and I'm taking an *a*pple.
Mark: I'm off to Europe and I'm taking a catapult.
Adam: No. I'm off to Europe and I'm taking an *a*crobat.
Catherine: I'm off to Europe and I'm taking a bicycle.
Adam: No. I'm off to Europe and I'm taking an *a*eroplane.
Mark: I'm off to Europe and I'm taking a *m*ushroom.
Adam: Yes.
Mark: Why?

Catherine: Oh, I see. I'm off to Europe and I'm taking a *c*amera.

Adam: Yes. I'm off to Europe and I'm taking an *a*nimal.

Mark: I'm off Europe and I'm taking a *d*og.

Catherine: No! I'm off to Europe and I'm taking *c*lothes pegs.

Adam: Yes – you've got it.

Mark: (probably) It's not fair!

Another version of this game is based on hobbies, games and trades, and the clue is not to use one letter of the alphabet, decided upon by the one in the know. It might go like this, supposing 'i' to be the taboo letter:

Catherine: I can play football.

Harriet: I can build.

Catherine: No. I can do photography.

Harriet: I can play croquet.

Catherine: Yes.

(But quite likely this was just a lucky shot on the part of Harriet, and there are still hours of gorgeous frustration ahead!)

Botticelli: this is really an adults' game, and is, to our knowledge, played daily by a compartment-full of businessmen travelling from Leeds to Manchester. However, it can obviously be played by older children, and even younger ones, if the challenger chooses a person that they would know about.

The challenger decides on a famous person, who may be fact or fiction, and tells the others the initial letter of that person's name (the name he is known by, therefore usually the surname, though in the case of Napoleon Bonaparte, either would be considered acceptable). The others try to discover his identity, but must do so by themselves fixing on some other well-known character, and framing the question in a sufficiently detailed way to enable the challenger to guess who is meant. If the challenger does not recognize who the questioner means, or gets it wrong, the questioner has a 'free' question, when he can ask anything he likes which can be answered 'Yes' or 'No' by the challenger. Thus, a game might go as follows:

Challenger: My name begins with B.
Questioner: Are you a deaf musician?
C: No, I am not Beethoven.
Q: Do you play football for a North of England team?
C: No. I'm not Georgie Best.
Q: Are you Alexander the Great's horse?
C: (long pause) I don't know what his name was.
Q: (triumphantly) Bucephalus. I get a free question. Are you a man?
C: Yes.
Q: Did you paint a picture of Venus rising from the sea?
C: Yes, I am Botticelli.

But it usually goes on for longer than that! And, note, that if the questioner had said merely 'Are you a painter?', the challenger would be quite within his rights to reply 'No, I am not Blake' – or Boudin or Bacon, or any other painter beginning with B – the questioner's question must be detailed enough to relate to only one particular person.

Chapter Six
The Passing Scene

Superstitions: there are various things you may see along the way which tradition says will bring you luck: two magpies; a chimney sweep; a black cat crossing your path; a white horse (provided that when you see it you all say 'Good luck to you, good luck to me, good luck to that white horse I see!'); the new moon (so long as you don't see it through glass; you should bow three times to it, and turn over your money, in the hope of doubling it before the month is out).

Distance: the players choose some object visible ahead in the distance, and guess how far away it is. The distance is checked on the milometer.

How Long is a Mile? At a given signal, the players close their eyes and estimate how long it takes to travel a mile, measured on the milometer. As each person thinks he has travelled a mile, he says 'Now!' The one who guesses nearest to the mile, either above or below is the winner. It is surprising how accurate you can become with practice. You can also play this game on a train, once you have identified the mileage marks by the line. Another variation is to guess how long is a minute, two minutes, or more.

Collecting: before you start this game you make a list of things which you may see by the road or railway. Your list should be of objects which it would be possible, though not too common, to see. Here are some suggestions: a caravan, a piebald horse, twins, an Alsatian dog, a crane. Whoever sees one of the things first scores a point. You may decide that some rarer objects earn more points. The winner is the one with the highest score in a given time. The game can also be played cooperatively, with the whole carload trying to see how many points they can get in a journey.

WHY DID THE ELEPHANT PAINT HIS TOENAILS RED?

SO HE WOULDN'T BE NOTICED WHEN HE CLIMBED UP THE CHERRY TREE.

I Spy: this can be the guessing game mentioned in the previous chapter, or you can compile lists of interesting categories of things seen, by using the 'I-Spy' books or compiling your own lists. You could make, say, a 'Nature' list in a little notebook thus:

Domestic Animal	*Tree*	*Flower*	*Bird*	*Wild Animal*
cat	oak	daisy	pigeon	rabbit
dog	ash	tulip	robin	hare
cow	larch	daffodil	pheasant	weasel

The lists could go on from trip to trip; you could try to set up records on a trip.

White Horse: two players or two teams of players take different sides of the road, and score points for animals seen. You may wish to award more points for unusual animals, and a White Horse scores 10. The animals can be alive or pictured on hoardings. One of the great White Horses scraped out of the chalk on the side of a hill scores 20! There are several – one in Kent, several in Wiltshire, one in Berkshire, one in Yorkshire – maybe more.

Animal Bingo: this game uses previously made-up 'Bingo' cards, all differing in content and/or order. A card might look like this:

CAT PIG LAMB	HEN DOG PHEASANT	HORSE COW SHEEP

Players check off each animal they see on their own side of the road (an animal crossing goes to the first one to call out). Again, you may include animals pictured on hoardings. The first person to complete a straight line across or down is the winner. This could also be played with other categories such as road signs, makes of cars or even with a mixture of objects (church, school, policeman, etc). Objects on these Bingo cards should be ones likely to be seen with reasonable frequency.

Inn Signs: two players or two teams take opposite sides of the road, and look out for inn signs with the name of creatures with legs. The winning team is the one with the highest score, in legs, on the journey. There are certain conventions; 22 is the highest score at any one time – this you would get for The Hare and Hounds for instance. The Coach and Horses is assumed to have 4 horses, that is 16 legs plus 2 more for the driver. You may or may not decide to allow 2 for such signs as The Queen's Arms (this means the Queen's coat of arms). In spite of the first rule above, our children are ever hopeful of coming across an inn called The Three Jolly Centipedes!

WHAT DO YOU GET IF YOU CROSS AN ELEPHANT WITH A GOLDFISH?

SWIMMING TRUNKS

Games with Car Numbers

These games are better not played where the traffic is very fast or, in some cases, very frequent.

Collecting Numbers: this game can be played over a single journey or over several, either competitively or cooperatively. The idea is to find numbers on licence plates in order from 1 upwards. It is much easier as you get into the 2- and 3-figure plates!

Counting from Number Plates: this game is confusing in heavy traffic, and is best played where you can see cars at frequent intervals, but not bunched up. The aim is to find the numbers from 1 to 25 embedded in the licence plates. The players take it in turn to look at the licence plates of passing cars. They may only score during their own turn. So a game might go:

Catherine: 453, no.
Mark: 712, yes, 1.
Adam: 348, no.
Catherine: 113, yes, 1.
Mark: 286, yes, 2.
Adam: Lucky you. 683, no. It's not fair!

Pick a Number: each player thinks of a number, of three figures, say 273, and then looks for it on passing car plates. One point is scored for an anagram of the number, as 732, or 237, and five points for the right number.

Pairs: each player is given a number from 1 to 9. They try to find licence plates with pairs of their number in them. 434 would count as being a pair of 4s just as well as 344. The winner is the first one to get ten pairs, or the one with the highest score in an agreed time.

Car Number Bingo: you can make 'cards' on pieces of paper as you travel. Each card is different, using different numbers up to 99 and/or different placings of the numbers. It is easier for the younger ones if the numbers go from lowest to highest. A card might look like this:

3	12	23	27
31	43	56	66
71	75	80	82
88	92	94	98

OR

3	31	71	88
12	43	75	92
23	56	80	94
27	66	82	98

The leader calls out numbers from passing cars' licence plates. If there is a reasonable flow of traffic he will call out the last two numbers, like this:

615 = 15 773 = 73 801 = 1

If, however, there is not much traffic, each licence plate can give two numbers, like this:

615 = 61 and 15 773 = 77 and 73 801 = 80 and 1

The players make a cross over any square on their card that contains a called number. There are various ways to determine the winner; the first one with a 'line' down or across, the first one to complete his card, the one with the most numbers in an agreed time. This game tends to have to go on until the last person has got his last number!

Licence Letters: the players take cars in turn, and try to make words using three letters of the licence plate in them, in the same order as they appear in the plate. Thus, for MRG one might have:

MaRkinG MaRGaret MaRketinG MeRGer MaRGate and so on.

One point is scored for each word. The winner is the one with the highest score in an agreed time.

You can also collect your name from licence plates, taking the letters out of different plates in order:

CAG gives C, HLD gives L, MDA gives A, TDR gives R, TBE gives E

(but note that had the third set of letters been ADR, A and R could have been used). This can be played competitively to see who can get his own name first – but it is obviously not fair if 'Henrietta' is playing against 'Clare'!

Identifying Car Makes: probably an easier game for boys than girls, as they usually take more interest in the subject. The real expert can also identify the vintage. The year on new licence plates is indicated by the final letter after the numbers: E = 1967, F = 1968, G = 1969, H = 1970, J = 1971, K = 1972. The car 'year' runs from August to August.

County of Origin: each county issues different letters for car licences, so you can tell by the licence plate of a car where it comes from. Players can take cars in turn, and try to spot ten different counties. The winner is the first to score ten. Lists of Index Marks (as these are called) appear in the Automobile Association and Royal Automobile Club handbooks.

Identifying Road Signs: The Highway Code shows all the road signs. Cooperatively or competitively, the players can see how many they can spot during the drive.

Who Lives There? get the driver to pause for a moment by a house, or choose one it takes time to pass.

Everybody draw on their observation and imagination to describe the house, and the people they think live in it. Or make a passing survey of a village or town. What sort of people live there? Mainly rich or poor? What do they do? How old is the place? What does its name mean? Why was it built there?

Chapter Seven
Take Pencil and Paper – Games for Trains

Most of these games are more suitable for trains than cars. Even usually good travellers may start to feel ill if they try to read or write in the car.

Noughts and Crosses: probably everyone knows this very old game, also called Tic-tac-toe. Two players draw a frame like Figure 1 (page 49), and take it in turns to enter a nought or a cross in the spaces, with the aim of being the first one to complete a line of their own symbol across, down or diagonally. In Figure 2 is a completed

frame in which the player using crosses is the winner.

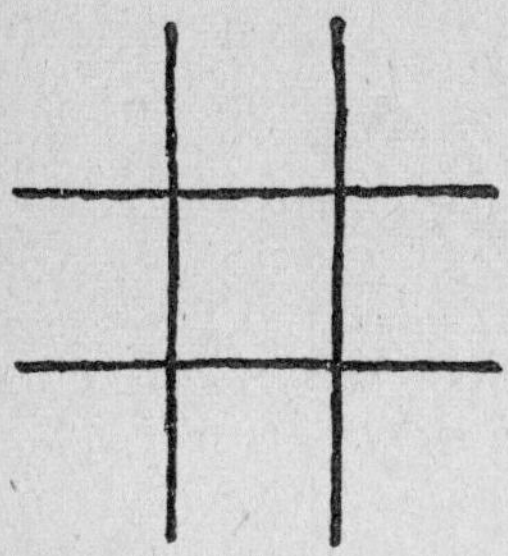

Fig. 1

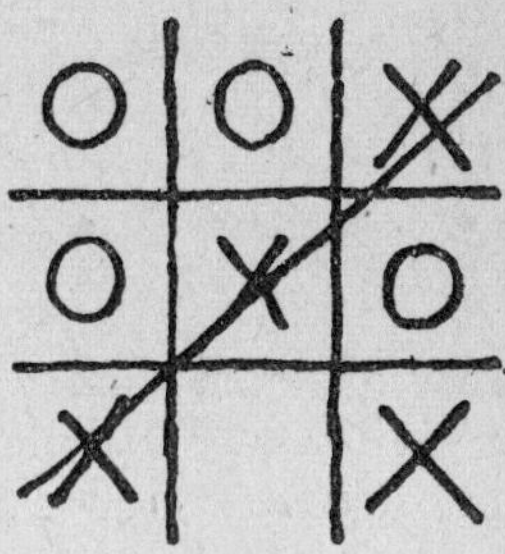

Fig. 2

Double Noughts and Crosses: this is a much more interesting development of the game. The two players start by drawing a frame of four interlocking noughts and crosses frames. They then play noughts and crosses either over the whole frame, as in Figure 3 below, or in one unit at a time, as in Figure 4. Either way the winner is the player with the largest number of his symbol in vertical, horizontal or diagonal lines of three.

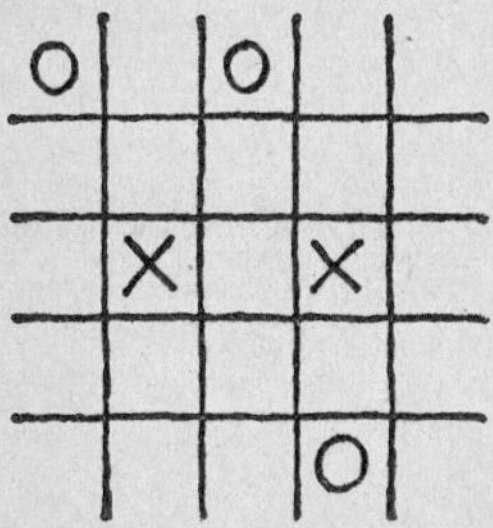

Fig. 3

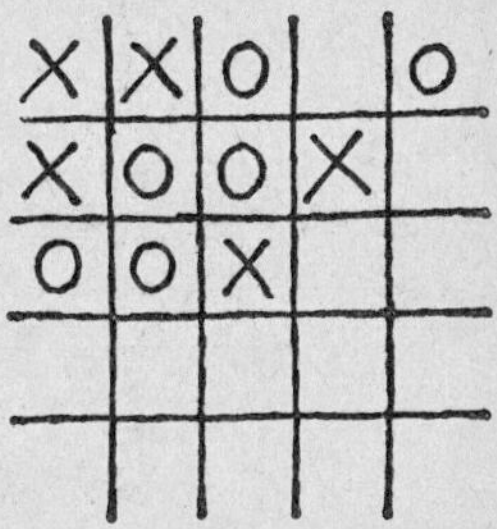

Fig. 4

Boxes: on a sheet of paper the players draw several lines of dots like this:

There is no set number of dots, the more there are the longer the game lasts. The aim of the game is to make boxes by joining up the dots, the one who completes the most boxes being the winner. Each player (usually two, but it is possible to play with three or four) takes it in turn to join any two dots vertically or horizontally. To prevent the opponent completing a box, a player avoids as long as possible drawing in the third side of a box. In the end, this becomes impossible, of course. The box belongs to the player who draws the fourth side, and who then puts his initial in it. The person who completes a box has another turn and can go on having more turns as long as he completes a box each turn. Here is what a game might look like part-way through:

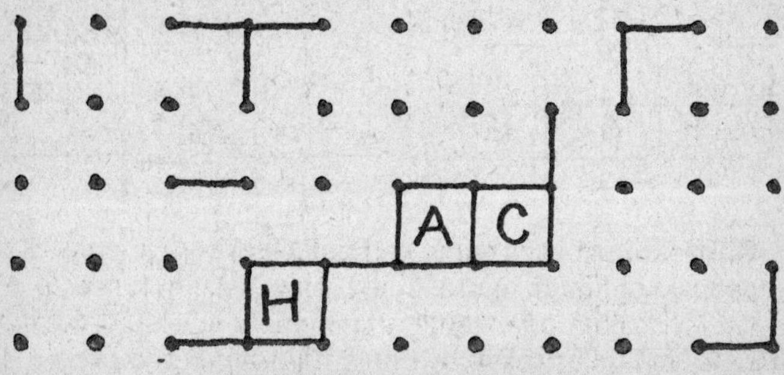

Drawing Blind: the players can all take part at once or take it in turns, which is probably more fun. The artist shuts his eyes and is told to draw an object, piece by piece, thus: 'Draw a pig. First draw its tail – now draw one front leg – now its body – now one back leg – now draw its head – now another back leg – now eyes – now the other front leg – now its ears. Now you can look!'

Other subjects which might be used are a house, a boat, other animals, a person, a person doing something like playing tennis or digging.

Number Maze: take a large sheet of paper and write 20 to 30 pairs of numbers, that is two 1s, two 2s, two 3s, etc, as in Figure 5. The first player draws a line joining any pair of numbers, as in Figure 6, and the others take it in turn to do the same. No line drawn must go through any other line, nor through any number. The player who cannot manage to join his chosen numbers without doing this must drop out of the game, until the last player left is the winner.

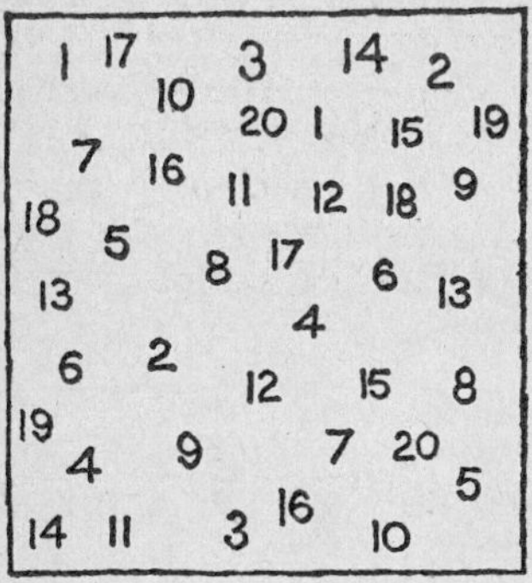

Fig. 5

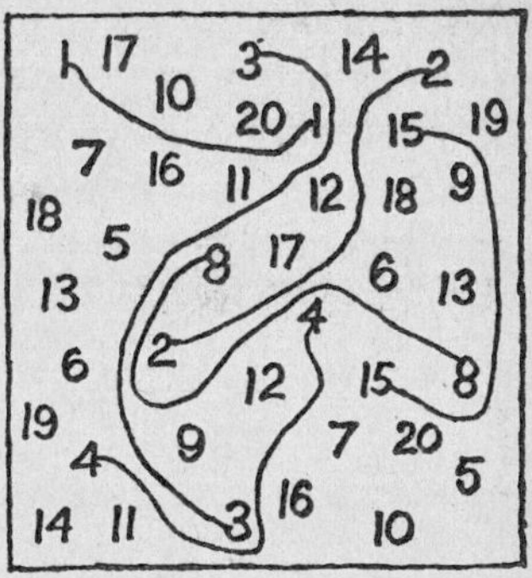

Fig. 6

Battleships: this game is best played with only two people, although more could play, taking turns in a circle, so that one would attack one's left-hand neighbour and be attacked by one's right-hand one.

First, each player draws two frames, each of twelve squares down and twelve across. The squares are then numbered across the top from 1 to 12, and the down squares are lettered from A to L. Onto one of his frames each player then places his 'fleet', which consists of:

One battleship which occupies 5 squares
Two battleships which occupy 3 squares each
Two battleships which occupy 2 squares each
One battleship which occupies 1 square

The ships may be drawn in any right-angled shape, but may not be on the diagonal. The players must not let their opponent see what they have drawn. A completed battle scene on a player's card might look like this:

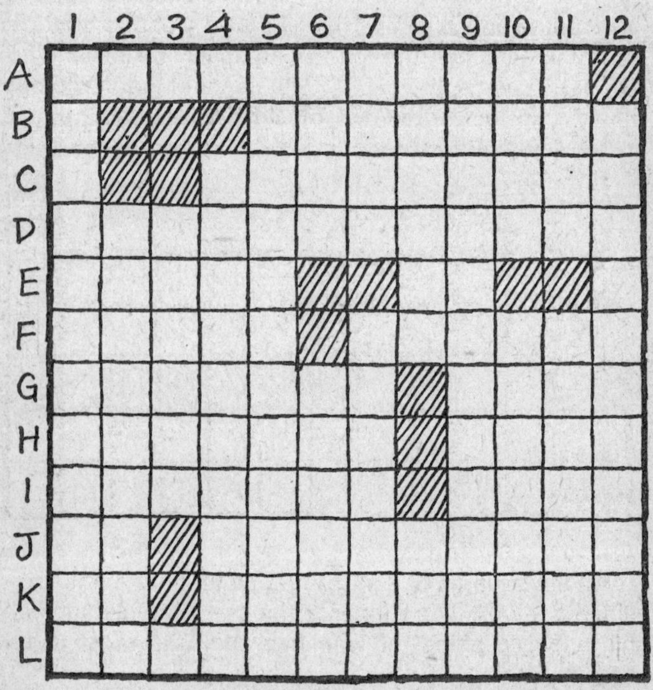

The players then try to sink each other's fleet. To do this, they take it in turn to call out the number of a square, as Al, B4, L6, H12, etc. To keep a record of their 'bombardment', as they call out the number of a square the players mark them off on their second frame, with a diagonal line for a miss, and a cross for a hit. So, after a few turns, the recording frame of the 'enemy' of the player above might look like this:

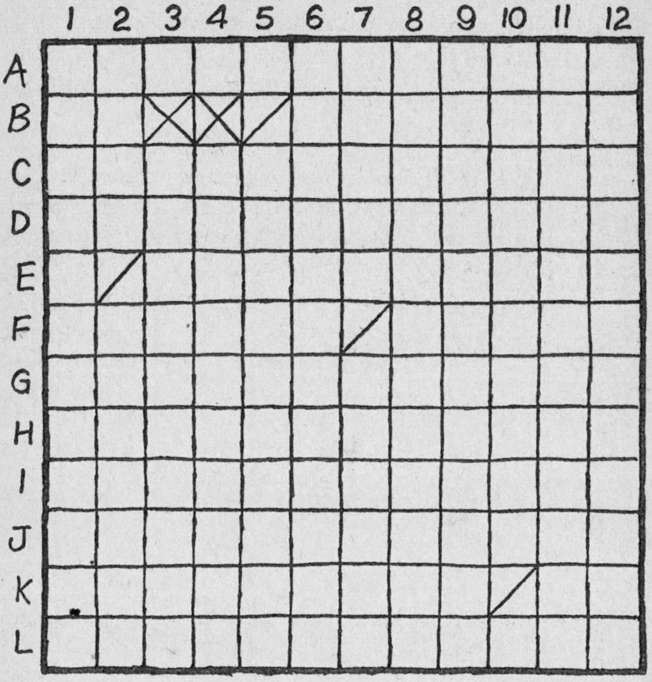

All the squares of a ship must be hit before it is considered 'sunk'. The winner is the one who has sunk all his enemy's ships, or who has sunk the most in an agreed time.

WHAT IS NAVY BLUE AND SWINGS FROM TREE TO TREE?

TARZAN IN A BOILER SUIT.

Drawing Inn Signs: one player draws an inn sign, such as The King's Head, The Fox and Hounds, The Goat in Boots; the others have to guess the pub's name, the correct guesser taking the next turn. This can also be played in two teams, with a leader telling a representative of each team the sign to be drawn, and the others on the team guessing. As soon as a sign is guessed the next team member goes to the leader to get the next sign. There should be at least as many signs as team members. The first team to have guessed all the signs is the winner.

Picture Words: there are various games you can play, representing words with pictures, numbers or letters. One is to write a sentence, a message or a letter using symbols wherever possible. A referee can decide which is the most ingenious and yet comprehensible contribution. Here are two examples:

I am in the car and I can see three trees and a cow.

Dear John,
Thank you for your letter. I am going to a football match with my father.

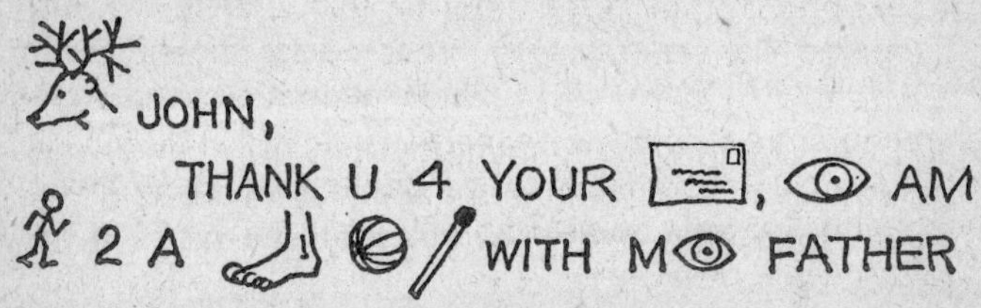

Another version is to give the players a list of place names which they have to represent in pictures. Some suggestions: Blackpool, Brixham, Castleford, Dorchester, Exmouth, Hampton, Oxford, Swansea, South Shields, Woodbridge.

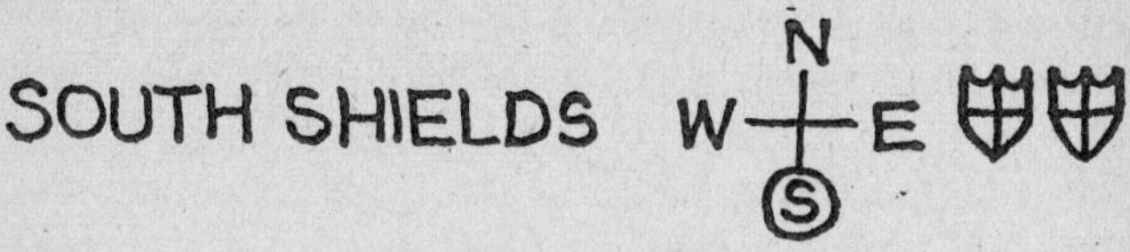

Beetle Drive: any number can play this game. A dice is needed, and paper and pencil for each player. The players take it in turn to throw the dice, with the aim of drawing a beetle according to the following list:

6 = body	5 = head	4 = a leg
3 = antenna	2 = an eye	1 = tail

A player may not begin until he has thrown a 6, but thereafter he can add the other parts in whichever order the dice falls (except that he cannot draw the eyes and antenna before his beetle has a head!). The winner is the one who completes his beetle first. (It is much easier if you have something flat, like a book or box lid, to throw the dice onto.)

Hangman: for any number of players. One player is the hangman. He chooses a word and writes it on his paper, not showing it to the others, and numbers each letter, like this:

T R A V E L L E R S
1 2 3 4 5 6 7 8 9 10

Then he tells the others how many letters there are in his word, and they make numbered spaces on their papers, like this:

\- - - - - - - - - -
1 2 3 4 5 6 7 8 9 10

Each player also draws a gallows like this by his word spaces:

Then the players take it in turn to suggest a letter. If that letter does indeed appear in the word chosen, the hangman tells them which space or spaces it fills, thus in 'travellers', R goes in 2 and 9. If a player suggests a wrong letter, or, when some of the letters are filled in, makes a guess at the whole word, and guesses wrongly, he draws part of a figure hanging on his gallows. He draws the head for the first wrong guess, the body for the next, and arms and legs for the next four. The loser is the player with his corpse nearest completion when the word is guessed, and anyone completely hung before the end of the game must drop out.

Constantinople or Words within a Word: a long word is chosen, and everyone writes down as many words as they can, using some of the letters of the chosen word. For instance, CONSTANTINOPLE contains at least:
constant; tin; pole; tan; none; an; in; cope; instant; stone; opal; on; onto; into; pin; pan; pen; sin; not; pot; cot – and many more.

The winner is the one with the longest list at the end of an agreed time.

Telegrams: a fairly long word is chosen. Each person tries to make up a telegram whose words begin with the letters of the selected word in order, thus:

RAILWAY
Roger and I lucky will aid you.

The winner is the most ingenious, as decided by the judge.

Sausages and Mash: for this game you need something to read. One person reads aloud to the others, and every time he comes to a word beginning with 's', he says 'sausages' instead, and, similarly, every word beginning with 'm' becomes 'mash'.

Consequences: each player has a piece of paper, and writes at the top an adjective describing a female. He then turns over the top to conceal his writing and passes it to his left-hand neighbour, taking his right-hand neighbour's paper, on which he writes a female name, turns it down and passes it on as before. Next are written in the same way an adjective describing a male, a male name, the place where the two met, what she said to him, what he said to her, what she gave him, what he gave her, what the consequence was, and what the world said. All the papers are then completely folded up, mixed together, and each person draws out one and reads it aloud, interspersing the appropriate linking words. I'm afraid that in families and among good friends, Consequences can be a very *rude* game. Here's an example of how it goes:

Cross-eyed Minnie Mouse *met* muscular Dr Who in a barrel going over Niagara Falls. *She said to him* 'Do you come here often?' *He said to her* 'Will you dance?' *She gave him* a tightrope. *He gave her* a plastic bucket. *The consequence was* he became President of the United States *and the world said* It's only what they deserved.

The Word Game or Penny's Game: played between two people. Each player privately decides on a 4- or 5-lettered word (as agreed) which must not have any repeated letters in it. This is written at the top of a piece of paper, and below it all the letters of the alphabet in sequence. The object of the game is to guess the opponent's word, the first one to guess being the winner. The method used is to take it in turn to suggest a 4- or 5-letter word, also with no repeated letters in it, to the opponent, who must then say how many, if any, of the letters of that word are in his chosen word. Gradually, by the thoughtful use of variants of words, letters are proved to be impossible, and are crossed off on the alphabet, or to be certainly in the opponent's word, and noted down accordingly. To keep a record you write down each word you have suggested, with the number of letters it had in it alongside. Best of all is if you are lucky enough to suggest a word which has none of your opponent's letters in it, so that you can eliminate all those letters at one fell swoop. Some words are very good as testing words, for instance TRUMP, upon which you may then try all sorts of one-letter variants, as FRUMP, TRAMP, CRUMP, to eliminate or establish other letters. It could, of course, happen for the word to be guessed quite by chance very early on, but, surprisingly, this seems hardly ever to happen. We must warn you that this game can gain itself fanatical devotees who then want to play it all the time.

Chapter Eight
A Cryptic Message

Here are various codes in which secret messages may be sent. The simplest is the two-line code. You write down the letters of the alphabet like this:

A B C D E F G H I J K L M
N O P Q R S T U V W X Y Z

Then, whenever you would normally write A you write N, for W use J and so on. Thus, in this code, COME HERE would be written PBZR URER.

A more secret version of this type of code is to use a 'password' in the first line, thus, when TRAVEL is the password:

T R A V E L B C D F G H I
J K M N O P Q S V W X Y Z

So COME HERE becomes SEAO YOKO, and only those who know the password can decipher it.

A slightly more complicated version is the four-line code which, if used with a password, works like this:

T R A V E L
B C D F G H
I J K M N O
P Q S U W X
Y
Z

Again the letter above or below the normal one is used, so that COME HERE is now RXUG LGCG.

A Code Dial: you can work out a similar sort of code with a code dial. To make this, you need to cut out two circles of paper, one about an inch larger in diameter than the other.

You divide each circle into 26 segments, and write the letters of the alphabet in order, one in each segment. (If you make 27 sections, you can include an ampersand – & – the sign of 'and', which means you need only use one letter to write 'and'.) You then fix the smaller circle on top of the larger with one of those paper clips which

spreads its legs out behind the paper, and makes the circles moveable. Now you decide on a 'key', for instance, that A = X, and set your dial so that the A on the top card is opposite the X on the lower one, and read off all the other letters accordingly. Thus COME HERE becomes ZIJB EBOB if read off the bottom card, or it could be FRPH KHUH if read off the top card. You can change the position of A in relation to the lower card whenever you like, and thus make hundreds of different codes.

The Rosecrucian Squares: another code system is known as the Rosecrucian Squares. To do this one, you first draw three lots of 'noughts and crosses' frames, and then write the alphabet into the frames like this:

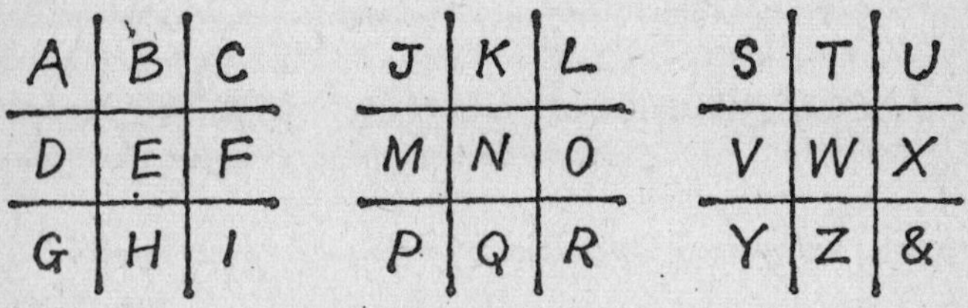

Then instead of writing letters, you make a hieroglyphic of their position in the frames. A is in the top left corner of the first frame, so it is represented by ; N is in the middle of the second frame, so it is shown as ; X is on the right side of the third frame in the middle, so it is represented by . Therefore, in the Rosecrucian Squares, COME HERE looks like this:

Again, as in the alphabet codes, you can have a password, so that the frames might look like this;

T	R	A	F	G	H	P	Q	S
V	E	L	I	J	K	U	W	X
B	C	D	M	N	O	Y	Z	&

and COME HERE would be like this: 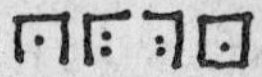

Alternatively, you can agree to start with a particular letter, in this case L:

L	M	N	U	V	W	C	D	E
O	P	Q	X	Y	Z	F	G	H
R	S	T	&	A	B	I	J	K

and COME HERE is now: 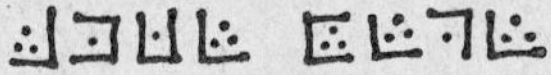

WHAT IS YELLOW AND SWINGS FROM CAKE TO CAKE?

TARZIPAN.

Chapter Nine
Cards on the Table

Most card games, especially played by more than two people, are only suitable for trains, in the open carriages with tables.

Old Maid: a game for three or more players. One of the Queens should be removed from the pack, leaving 51 cards, then all the cards are dealt round. Each player looks at his hand and takes out any pairs he finds, such as two 2s, two Jacks, etc. These cards are stacked all together in the centre of the table. The player on the left of the dealer begins, by offering his cards, faces hidden, to his left-hand neighbour. This player takes one, and if it makes a pair with a card in his hand, lays the pair down; otherwise he adds the card to his hand. He then offers his cards to his left-hand neighbour, and so on round the circle, until eventually only one player is left with a card unpaired – one of the Queens, the Old Maid.

Snap: any number of players. The cards are all dealt round, and each player piles his own cards face *down* beside him. The player on the left of the dealer begins, by placing his top card face *up* in the middle of the table; then the next player on the left puts a card face up on the top of the first card, and so on round the circle. If a card being put down is the same as the card before (both Aces, threes, fives, etc), the player who manages to shout 'Snap' first takes the whole pile, which he puts face down under his own pile. Anyone who runs out of cards drops out of the game, and the winner is the one who gets the whole pack, or who has the most cards at the end of an agreed time. Some people add the refinement that if two people call 'Snap' absolutely together, the pile goes to neither, but is put on one side. Then if a pair to the top card on this pile comes up on the main pile, the first player to call 'Snap pool' takes the lot.

Animal Snap: this is played just like ordinary Snap, but each player is told he is a different animal, such as cow, dog, cat, owl, lion, and has to make his appropriate noise instead of shouting 'Snap'.

Donkey in the Yard: all the cards are dealt out. The object of the game is to collect four of a kind (four Aces, four Queens, four 10s, etc). Each player looks at his own hand, and then all at the same time, each player passes a card of his own choice to the player on his left, face-*down*. When a player has four of a kind in his hand, he lays his hand down quietly on the table, then puts his hands to his head like a donkey's ears. When the other players see this, they must do likewise, and the last one to get his hands up is a part 'donkey'. A player who comes last three times is 'Donkey in the Yard' and drops out of the game. The game continues until all but one of the players is eliminated. When the game gets down to only a few players, some of the sets of four can be removed, to make the hands easier to manage.

Pelmanism: any number of players. The cards are all spread out in a random way face down. In turns, each player chooses two cards, and turns them face upwards, for long enough for the other players to see what they are. If they are a pair, he takes them, if not he turns them down again in the *same* position they were in before. If a player gets a pair he gets another turn; no player may have more than three turns in a row. The winner is the person who makes the most pairs, that is, who remembers best the position of cards formerly turned up which match the ones he turns up.

Mao-Mao: this is a French game for any number of players. The cards in each suit from 2 to 5 are taken out, leaving 36 cards. Each player is dealt four cards, the rest are put face *down* in the middle of the table, then the top card is put face *up* beside the pile. The players look at their cards. The player to the left of the dealer begins, by putting down on the exposed card in the centre, either a card of the same value (ten on ten, for instance) or the same suit (eg, diamond on diamond). If he can do neither, he picks up a card from the common pack. If a Queen is put down, the next player must pick up two cards from the common pack instead of taking his normal turn; if the Jack is put down, the next player loses his turn. The winner is the one who gets rid of all his cards first.

Knock: three or more players. Each player is dealt seven cards. The remaining pack is put face *down* in the middle, with the top card exposed beside it. The game is then played the same as Mao-Mao, except that instead of the Jack and Queen changing what people have to do, if a player puts down a 2 or a 3, the next player must pick up a card from the common pack; if a 7 is put down the next player misses his turn; if an 8 is played, the direction of play is altered, now going from left to right, until the next 8 is played, when it reverses again. When a player has only two cards left in his hand, he must knock on the table before playing the first of them, and if he forgets to do so, he must pick up a card instead. The first one to get rid of all his cards is the winner, but play continues until there is only one person left.

Beggar my Neighbour: a game for only two players. A game may only last ten minutes or it can go on all day, entirely according to the way the cards fall, and not the will of the players. All the cards are dealt out; each player has his hand face *down* beside him. The players take it in turn to turn a card face up on the table to make a pile between them. They continue to do this until one player turns up a picture card. His opponent then has to 'pay' him by placing the following number of cards on the common pack:

For a Jack – one
for a Queen – two
for a King – three
for an Ace – four

If one of the payment cards is a picture card, the payer

stops paying and the other player must pay him. When a full payment has been made without interruption, the payee takes the whole pile and places it face down at the bottom of his own hand. A hand might go like this:

> Mark plays 2, Harriet plays 4, Mark plays Ace, Harriet 'pays' 3, 7, 10 and Queen, Mark pays King, Harriet pays 8, 5, 9, and Mark picks up the pile.

The winner is the one who manages to get the whole pack, or who has the greatest number of cards at the end of an agreed time.

Fish: two or more players. Each player is dealt seven cards, the remainder of the pack is put in the middle, face *down*. The players look at their hands and sort them into cards of equal value. The aim is to make up complete sets of four. The player on the dealer's left asks his left-hand neighbour for a card – he does not specify the suit, only the value; and he must have at least one card of this value already in his hand. His neighbour must give him all the cards he holds of that value. If the player's request is successful, he gets another turn, if not, his neighbour says 'Fish', and he must take the top card from the common pack. Once a player gets a set of four, he must use up his next turn in putting them down on the table. The first person to get rid of all his cards is the winner.

Sans Aces or No Aces: another French game for up to four players. Each player is dealt 13 cards, and any remaining cards are put away, and not used in the game. The players sort out their hands into the order of value, ignoring suit. Aces count as 1. The player on the left of the dealer puts down on the table an Ace, if he has one, followed by other cards in consecutive order for as long as he can. When he has not got the appropriate card he says 'No threes' (or whatever the missing card is, possibly even 'No Aces'), and the next player takes over from where the first one left off, for as long as *he* can. If none of the players has a particular card, that number is skipped, and the next one is tried. The player who puts down the King starts a new sequence, but he may start it wherever it suits him best to do so, to aid in getting rid of his cards. The one who finishes all his cards first is the winner.

Sevens: three or more players. The pack is all dealt round. Everybody looks at his hand and sorts it out into suit and sequence. The person who holds the 7 of diamonds begins the game, by putting it down in the middle of the table. The next player, if possible, puts down the 6 or 8 of diamonds on one side of the 7. If he has neither, but has a 7 of another suit, he puts that down above the 7 of diamonds. If he can do nothing he 'passes'. The object of the game is to get the cards piled up in suits, 6 down to Ace on one side of each seven, and 8 up to King on the other side. The winner is the one to get rid of all his cards first. There is a certain devious skill in withholding key cards as long as possible, but a player must never pass if he has a card he can play, no matter how disadvantageous to himself. It is possible to play 'Sevens' with only two people, if the 7 of diamonds is first put on the table and then a third 'dummy' hand dealt, which the players pick up from instead of passing.

Vingt-et-Un or Pontoon: this is really a gambling game, but can perfectly well be played without wagers. The players first cut the pack to decide who shall be dealer. The one who gets the highest card wins, Aces being counted as 1. Each player is dealt two cards, including the dealer. Everyone except the dealer looks at his own hand. The aim is for one's cards to add up to 21 – picture cards counting as 10, aces as 11. If a player is *dealt* with cards which add up to 21, he declares it at once, saying 'Vingt-et-un' or 'Pontoon' and showing his hand, and a new game begins. The winner becomes the new dealer. If nobody has 21 right away, the player on the left of the dealer begins. He looks at his cards and makes up his mind whether to say 'Stick', if he feels another card may make his score over 21, or, if he wants to take that risk, (and he must, if the cards in his hand add up to 14 or less) to say 'twist', whereupon the dealer gives him a card face up. If this card makes his score over 21, he says 'Bust', and the next player has his turn. If not, he makes up his mind again whether to 'stick' or 'twist'. Once he 'sticks' the next player has his turn. When it comes to the dealer's turn, he turns his hand face up, so that everyone can see it, and plays it according to the same rules. The winner is the player with the hand which either reaches 21, or is the nearest to 21 but below.

Three Patiences

Round the Clock: twelve cards are laid out face down on the table, in the shape of a clock face; the thirteenth card is placed face down in the centre. Again twelve cards are put face down on the first twelve and the thirteenth in the middle, and so on until all the cards are down. The last card to be put in the centre is then turned up, and put into its appropriate position on the clock face – three at three o'clock, Queen at twelve o'clock, etc – under the down-turned cards; the top card of that pile is then turned up and played. If a King is turned up he goes in the centre. The game is won if all the cards can be put round the clock before the fourth King appears.

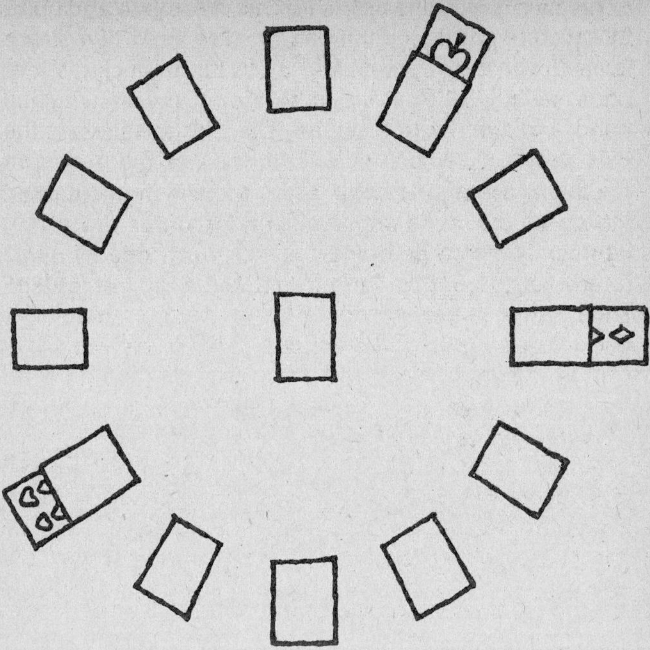

Four Aces: the aim of this patience is to be left with the four aces only on the table. Four cards are laid out side by side. If there are two or more cards of the same suit exposed, the lower numbers are discarded; Aces are high. Having discarded everything possible, four more cards are laid on the first cards or spaces, and the same procedure followed. An Ace can be moved into a space, but no other card can be. The game ends when all the cards have been gone through once.

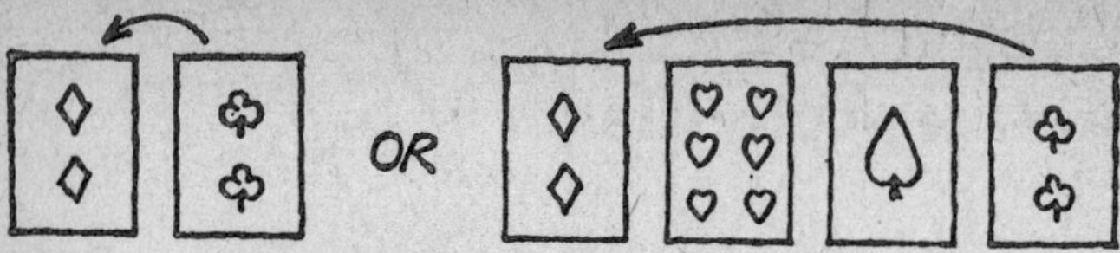

Side by Side or One over Two: the aim in this game is to get all the cards in one pile on top of the first card laid down. The cards are laid out in a row one by one. A card can be put on top of another of the same suit or the same value, but only if it is either immediately next to its pair, or if there are two cards in between.

Chapter Ten
Active Activities

1. While Stationary

Here are some suggestions for games that can be played at stops on a car journey, so that you can stretch your legs and work off energy. Be sure you play safely away from the road.

Follow my Leader: all form up in a line behind one of the players and follow him, copying his actions, which should be as peculiar and eccentric as possible.

The Dove and the Hawk: a game for three players. One is the dove, one the hawk, and the third the owner. The owner stands between the other two, holding onto their hands. He lets the dove fly off, fluttering his hand to show it has been let out. The dove runs around, flapping his arms like a flying bird. When the owner thinks he has had enough start, he releases the hawk. The hawk, also flapping, must follow the same route as the dove. When the owner decides they have been flying long enough, he claps his hands for them to return. The hawk tries to catch the dove before he gets back to the owner (remember he *must* follow the dove's route). If the dove is caught, he becomes the hawk, the hawk becomes the owner, and the owner becomes the dove. If the dove gets to safety without being caught, the dove becomes the owner, the hawk becomes the dove, and the owner becomes the hawk.

What's the Time, Mr Wolf? One player takes the part of Mr Wolf, and wanders about, while the other players follow after him. Every now and then one says 'What's the time, Mr Wolf?' and so long as he answers by saying it is such and such o'clock, they are safe, but when he answers 'Dinner-time!' everyone must dash for 'home' before he catches him. Anyone caught becomes Mr Wolf for the next turn.

Shadow Tag: one player is 'He', and tries to catch one of the others by stepping on his shadow. This one then becomes He.

Cross Tag: everybody mills about, and the He calls out the name of one of the players, and then chases him. If another player crosses between pursuer and pursued, He must chase that person instead, and so on until someone is caught.

French Tag: the first He just has to catch one of the others by touching some part of his body. This person then becomes He but must keep one hand on the part touched, until he touches one of the others. If he has been touched on the foot he must hop.

Everybody Cross: the He stands between two lines about 15 feet apart. The players must get across from one line to the other without being caught, when He calls out '1, 2, 3, everybody cross'. Anyone caught stays to help He until the last one left free is the winner.

Leap Frog: one player makes a 'back', by bending forward with his hands firmly grasping his shins, and his head tucked well in. Another player then takes a short run up to him, puts his hands on his back and jumps over him, with legs spread wide apart. This player then runs on a little way and makes a 'back' in his turn. The next player jumps over both, and so on.

Pig in the Middle: this game is for three players and a ball. Of course, this game or any other ball game should not be played at the side of the road, but only in a field or somewhere away from the road. The players stand in a row as far apart as they choose. The two end players then throw the ball to each other, while 'Pig' tries to catch it. When he does, the one who threw the ball becomes 'Pig'.

Exercises: any that you can think of. Some suggestions are: touching toes then stretching up as far as you can, arms stretched out too; running or jumping on the spot; jumping with arms and legs spread wide and together alternately; hopping, skipping, and jumping; hopping like a frog or a rabbit.

2. While Travelling

O'Grady Says: this game can be used for some controlled stretching and movement which will not elbow the driver, or kick the back of his seat.

The leader is O'Grady. The others must obey his instructions if he says '*O'Grady says* do so-and-so', but they must do nothing if he merely says 'Do so-and-so'. If a player obeys when he should not have, he loses one of his three lives, and returns to his previous position. Here is how a game might go:

O'Grady says put your hands on your head.
O'Grady says turn your head to the right.
Drop your hands.
O'Grady says drop your hands.
Turn your head back.
O'Grady says turn your head to the left – and so on.

Another version of this game is 'Do this, do that'. In this one, the players follow the leader's example when he says 'Do this', but do nothing when he says 'Do that'.

Coordination: here are three games to test your coordination.

1. Hold your left ear with your right hand, and your nose with your left hand. At a command change over the hands.
2. With your right hand rub your stomach with a circular movement, while with your left hand you pat yourself on the head.
3. Hold both arms out in front of you. Cross them at the wrist, and interlace your fingers, palms together and thumbs at the bottom. Now bring your hands up, against your chest, and under your chin. Thumbs will now be outermost. One of the other players now points to any one of your fingers and tells you to move it. It is surprisingly difficult to get the right one.

Finger Throwing: two players face each other, with one hand clenched in front of them. At a count of three, each player puts out his hand, either spreading out some or all of his fingers, or keeping it clenched. As they do this they also guess aloud how many fingers their opponent will show. The winner is the one to make 5 correct guesses first.

Fist and Hand: two players sit opposite each other, with a small, smooth object (a pebble, a sweet, a dice, etc) between them. The players, in turn, and quickly and rhythmically, place a hand flat on the object. Then one player picks up the object, and now they must put a clenched fist where the object was, until the player puts the object down again, when once more they change to flat hands. A player loses one of his three lives if he does the wrong thing with his hand, putting his fist on the object or a flat hand on the empty space. To be effective the movement must be fast and unhesitating, so that it gets into a pattern which it is difficult to break when the object changes its position.

Scissors, Stone, Paper: this game uses the following symbols:

Scissors = index and third fingers extended
Stone = clenched fist
Paper = flat hand

Two players face each other, each with one fist in full view in front of him – on a table if there is one, or on his knees. They both thump their fists up and down three times and then simultaneously make one of the symbols with it. The winner of each round is the one whose symbol 'overcomes' the other's: thus, scissors, cut paper, but are broken by stone; stone breaks scissors but can be wrapped in paper; paper can wrap stone, but is cut by scissors. If both show the same symbol, it is a tie. The game continues until an agreed score is reached, or an agreed number of lives lost.

3. Things to Make or Play With

Making Paper Chains: a good occupation on your way to a Christmas holiday. Use the pre-stuck chains one can buy at Woolworths, have a damp sponge in a plastic bag, and a basket to pile the chains in as they are finished.

Hand Puppets and Finger Puppets: make your own before the journey from old socks or mittens, with drawn or embroidered features; or on the spot from a paper bag or (even more basic) draw a face on your palm, with a felt-tip pen – just two eyes, a nose and a mouth. By creasing your hand you can make different expressions. Impromptu plays can then be enacted. A face drawn on each finger provides the actors for a crowd scene.

Practising Knots: it is very useful to everybody to be able to tie other knots beside dear old Granny, as any Boy Scout knows. Here are a few that often come in handy:

Slip Knot: used to pull a string tight before knotting it round something securely, also for lassos.

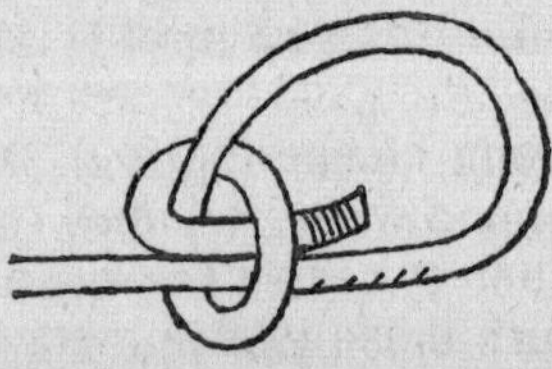

Reef Knot: this knot won't slip, unties easily and is the best knot for tying up parcels.

Clove hitch: to tie your boat to a bollard, your horse outside the saloon; either end will take a strain without slipping, lengthways and downwards.

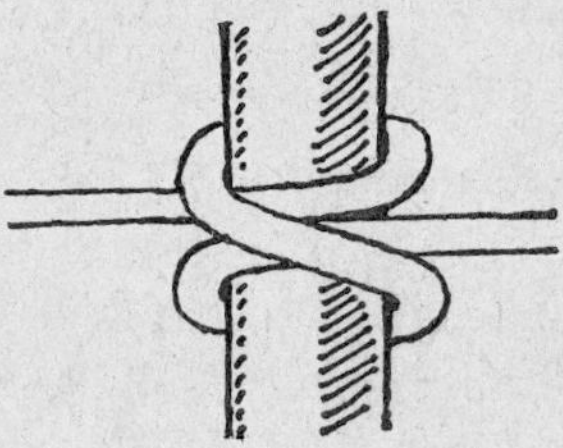

Sheet bend: for joining two ropes of unequal thickness together – immensely useful when you have two quite different bits of string, neither quite long enough to do up your parcel.

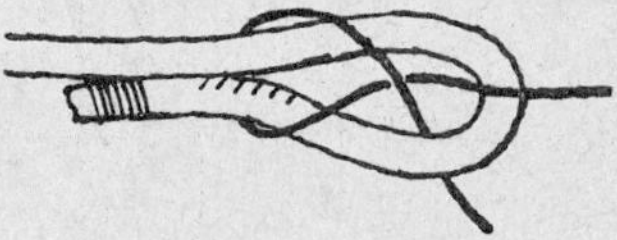

Paper Fortune Teller: you need a square piece of paper. Fold it in quarters and crease it well on the folds. Open out again and crease the four corners into the centre. Turn over and write 'fortunes' round the edges (can be descriptions of people you will marry, or events to befall you). Turn these four corners into the centre and crease, then write in numbers on the flaps as shown. Fold in half, open and fold in half the other way. Put your two thumbs and two forefingers inside the flaps facing you. By moving your fingers and thumbs you can open the pyramids so formed in two directions; one way shows numbers 1 to 4 and the other numbers 5 to 8.

The fortune teller then asks one of the others to choose a number between 1 and 4, and opens and shuts the pyramids that number of times. Then he is asked to choose one of the numbers now showing, and again the pyramids are opened and shut that many times. Again he chooses from one of the numbers showing, and this time the flap with that number on is turned back, and his fortune read.

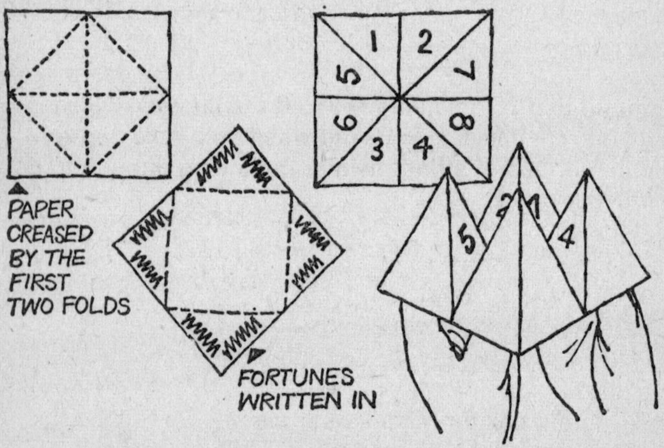

Chapter Eleven
Songs and Poems

Sing Songs: everyone sings – nursery rhymes, pop songs, round songs, songs learnt at school and, on Christmas journeys, Christmas carols.

Round Songs: here are a few to remind you. One person sings the first line of the song, then while he sings the second line the next person starts on the first line, and so on until everyone is singing.

Frère Jacques
Frère Jacques, Frère Jacques,
Dormez-vous? Dormez-vous?
Sonnez les matines, sonnez les matines.
Ding dang dong, ding dang dong!

Or the same song in English:
Are you sleeping? Are you sleeping?
Brother John, Brother John.
Ring the bell for Matins, ring the bell for Matins,
Ding dang dong, ding dang dong!

Fire's Burning:
Fire's burning, fire's burning,
Draw nearer, draw nearer,
In the gloaming, in the gloaming,
Come sing and be merry.

Canoe Song:
Row, row, row the boat,
Gently down the stream,
Merrily, merrily, merrily, merrily,
Life is but a dream.

WHAT IS WHITE AND CRUMBLY AND SWINGS THROUGH THE TREES?

A MERINGUE-UTANG.

A–Z Singing: sing a song, either together or in turn, for each letter of the alphabet. The title of each song has to start with the letters of the alphabet in sequence. For instance:

All Things Bright and Beautiful
Baa Baa, Black Sheep
Come Lasses and Lads
Drink to Me Only with Thine Eyes
For Auld Lang Syne

IF YOU WAKE UP IN THE MORNING AND FIND AN ELEPHANT IN YOUR BED, HOW DO YOU KNOW HE IS AN ELEPHANT?

BECAUSE OF THE E EMBROIDERED ON HIS PYJAMA JACKET

Action Songs: you can make up mimes to go with any suitable song. You'd better watch out that the actions don't get so uninhibited that you look as though you were travelling with a cartload of monkeys; and keep well clear of the driver! Here is one traditional action song:

John Brown's Baby:
John Brown's baby (fold arms and rock them)
Had a cold (cough)
Upon its chest (slap chest)

Repeat this twice, then –

So they rubbed him (rub chest)
With camphorated oil (hold nose)

Needless to say, this is sung to the tune of *John Brown's Body*, or more properly of *The Battle Hymn of the Republic.*

Singing Bee: Each person in turn sings a song or a verse of a song. The others may join in the chorus.

Here are two examples of songs with plenty of verses!

London Bridge Is Falling Down:

London Bridge is falling down,
Falling down, falling down,
London Bridge is falling down,
My fair lady.

Build it up with wood and clay,
Wood and clay, wood and clay,
Build it up with wood and clay,
My fair lady.

Wood and clay will wash away, etc.
Build it up with bricks and mortar, etc.
Bricks and mortar will not stay, etc.
Build it up with iron and steel, etc.
Iron and steel will bend and bow, etc.
Build it up with silver and gold, etc.
Silver and gold will be stolen away, etc.
Set a man to watch all night, etc.
Suppose the man should fall asleep, etc.
Give him a pipe to smoke all night, etc.

Hush, Little Baby:

Hush, little baby, don't say a word,
Papa's gonna buy you a mocking bird.

If that mocking bird don't sing,
Papa's gonna buy you a diamond ring.

If that diamond ring is brass,
Papa's gonna buy you a looking-glass.

If that looking-glass gets broke,
Papa's gonna buy you a billy-goat.

If that billy-goat don't pull,
Papa's gonna buy you a cart and bull.

If that cart and bull turn over,
Papa's gonna buy you a dog called Rover.

If that dog named Rover don't bark,
Papa's gonna buy you a horse and cart.

If that horse and cart fall down,
You're still the prettiest little baby in town,
You're still the prettiest little baby in town.

Learning poems: someone who knows a poem can teach it to the others, or you could have a book, either a selection of poems or something like Edward Lear's *A Book of Nonsense* or A.A. Milne's *Now We Are Six.*

Reciting poems: this can follow on from the last or be done on its own. Each person takes turns to recite a poem, either learnt or made up by themselves.

Limericks: you can make up your own limericks quite easily because they have a set form, like these:

There was an old man of Peru,
Who found a large rat in his stew,
Said the waiter, 'Don't shout
And wave it about,
Or the rest will be wanting one too!'

There was an old man of Khartoum,
Who kept two black sheep in his room.
'They remind me,' he said,
'Of two friends who are dead,
But I cannot remember of whom.'

Chapter Twelve

Games for Your Little Brother and Sister

Before the journey you can make some preparations to keep your little brother or sister amused.

Lucky Dip: there are various ways of organizing a lucky dip. You can have a collection of items in a draw-string bag or a box which can be 'dipped' into. (If there is more than one small child it is best for them to take it in turns, so that the surprise is everyone's surprise.) Or you can hand out a surprise yourself from a bag of your own; or you can wrap up little parcels which can be 'dipped' for from a basket or punnet. The parcels should be wrapped in different-coloured paper to show whom they are for. You need not have a new lucky dip each time you travel. Keep the lucky dip for journeys, collecting the items back at the end of each journey, but each time you travel it is a good idea to add a few new items and take away a few familiar ones. But you must be sure, if this is to be a success, that the lucky dip bag is kept only for journeys and special occasions.

Here are a few suggestions for what to put in the lucky dip:

Sweets wrapped separately or in sufficient quantity for everyone to have one;
Small toys;
A little notebook;
Coloured pencils;
Small picture books;

A small jigsaw puzzle;
A padlock and key;
A small game like solitaire or a maze;
A paper hat;
A tape measure;
A magnet;
A magnifying glass.

Pass the Parcel: another variation on Lucky Dip is the game of Pass the Parcel. Wrap up an object in layer upon layer of paper and string. Each person in turn takes off one layer or piece of string. To prolong the pleasure you may decide that a layer may only be taken off when agreed landmarks are passed or the next milestone reached. The last person to take off a wrapper keeps the prize, or this may be sweets which can be divided between all the players. Alternatively, you can wrap a small surprise between each layer of paper, so that each time the parcel is passed, the players find something. For this variation, you need to ration the time for the appearance of each new surprise. If there isn't a surprise between *every* sheet, a special coloured paper could signal the appearance of the next surprise.

Story telling: most children will listen happily to stories for as long as the storyteller's voice holds out. Make up your own or tell the traditional tales you know well, such as 'Red Riding Hood', 'The Three Bears', 'Cinderella', etc.

Finger Games: these are games with words or actions. *Round and Round the Garden*: hold the child's hand, palm upwards, in yours. With two fingers 'walk' round the palm, saying: 'Round and round the garden walks the Teddy bear, one step (up the wrist) two steps (up the arm) and tickle you under there (right up under the arm).

Here's the Church: 'Here's the church' (hands held up, palms facing and the fingers interlaced inside the palms). 'And here's the steeple' (the forefingers are brought out and held upright, with the tips touching each other). 'Look inside and see all the people' (turn the hands over so the fingers show and wiggle them). 'Here's the parson going upstairs' (bend right thumb down to the little fingers and 'climb' up all the fingers). 'And here's the parson saying his prayers' (hands are clasped again with the right thumb appearing at a 'window' or 'pulpit' between the left thumb and forefinger).

Incy Wincy Spider: this is a verse with gestures.

Incy wincy spider	Hands are held a little apart, palms facing.
Climbed the waterspout.	Put the tips of the little fingers together, then turn the hand to put the next fingertips together, little ones coming apart, and so on until the thumbs come together.
Down came a raindrop And washed the spider out.	Gesture with both hands downwards and outwards.
Out came the sunshine And dried up all the rain.	Rays of sun are mimed with outspread fingers and hands.
Incy wincy spider Climbed the spout again.	As for the first verse.

Nursery Rhymes: recite or sing all the nursery rhymes you know.

I'm Thinking of Something Red: this is a version of 'I Spy' (see page 34) which can be played by children who know their colours but do not yet know their letters. One player says, 'I'm thinking of something red' (or green or yellow or whatever), and the others have to guess what it is. It can be restricted to something you can see as in 'I Spy', or it could be anything anywhere.

Look at Me: try to make someone laugh by gazing into his or her eyes. You can make all sorts of grimaces; if agreed, you may speak, but you must not look away at all. The one able to hold out longest without laughing, or smiling, is the winner.

Pass the Laugh: this is another game in which a smile or a laugh eliminates you. Players take turns to 'pass the laugh', each adding one as they do so. So it goes like this:

Harriet: Ha.
Catherine: Ha, ha
Mark: Ha ha ha.
Adam: Ha ha ha ha.

And all must keep a straight face or drop out.

Chapter Thirteen
Making Your Own Picnic

Many families have picnic customs of their own, but here are a few ideas to remind you or give you new picnic ways, if you are going on a long journey and will have to stop for food or if you are going somewhere by car to have a picnic.

THINGS TO TAKE

Plates or bowls and cups
These can either be unbreakable or you can use the polystyrene trays that fruit and vegetables are packed in at supermarkets for plates and yoghurt or cream cartons for cups. The advantage of these is that you can throw them straight in the dustbin when you get home, so there is no washing up. But please *don't* throw them away on the roadside to make it ugly and dirty for other people who come after you. Even if the people who have been there before you have behaved badly with their rubbish, you don't have to follow their horrible example!

Cutlery
This can be plastic, but you will probably need one knife that cuts properly.
Paper napkins
Salt, pepper and sugar in little screwtop bottles
Tin opener
Bottle opener

And now to the food!

Here are some suggestions for the sort of food you can take on a picnic and some recipes of things you may like to make yourself for a picnic.

Bread and butter or rolls and butter (so you can make your own sandwiches or eat them with other food).

Lettuce, tomatoes, watercress, radishes, raw carrots, raw cauliflower (rather nice and quite different from cooked).

Salad cream.

Potato salad (see the recipe).

Risotto (see the recipe).

Hard-boiled eggs.

Meat pies, cornish pasties, sausage rolls, vol-au-vents.

Frankfurters (remember to take some mustard!).

Nuts, raisins, crisps.

Cheese.

Cake, biscuits, buns.

Shortbread (see the recipe).

Apples, bananas, oranges, grapes and other fruit in season.

Fruit salad in a plastic bowl with a lid.

Bottles of water, squash, milk.

Thermos of tea or coffee and soup.

Here are some suggestions for sandwiches. Remember the best sandwiches are the ones that have the most inside them.

Peanut butter with jam or honey or tomato sauce or lettuce.

Scrambled eggs with or without mayonnaise.

Crisp bacon and tomato.

Sardine mashed with vinegar or lemon juice.

Tuna fish with mayonnaise or lemon juice.

Cottage cheese with chives or chopped cucumber or gherkins or jam.

Cheese and chutney.
Mashed banana, possibly with chopped walnuts.
Ham and lettuce.
Chicken and lettuce or minced chicken and mayonnaise.

RECIPES

Potato Salad

Mix some cold mashed potato with mayonnaise so that it tastes right to you. Add to it chopped chives or chopped raw onion (not too much!). Put it in a plastic bowl which has a lid and sprinkle it with red pepper or paprika before closing the lid.

Risotto

Ask your mother to cook enough rice for the family. As soon as it is cooked and drained, mix in one or two items from each of these lists:

chopped chives	diced chicken
¼ lb packet garden peas (thawed but not cooked)	shrimps, either from a tin or frozen
2 tomatoes cut into small pieces	crisp cooked bacon
diced cooked beans	chopped ham
a tin of sweetcorn, drained	chopped almonds
raisins or sultanas	chopped hard-boiled egg

Have everything ready for mixing, so the rice will stay hot. When it is all mixed together, put the risotto into one of those wide-mouthed vacuum jars and put the lid on firmly. The heat from the rice will cook and warm the things you have mixed in on the way to the picnic.

If you like it, you can mix in some curry powder (about ½ teaspoon to each pound of rice) to give it colour and extra taste. Don't forget to take a serving spoon with a long handle!

Shortbread

Have ready two round tins 6 inches across. Heat your oven to 325° (electric) or Mark 3 (gas).

Beat 2 ounces caster sugar (¼ cup) into 4 ounces (½ cup) slightly softened (not melted) butter. Cream them together well, until the mixture is white and light and the sugar no longer feels gritty.

Mix in 8 ounces (1½ cups) plain flour and a pinch of salt.

Mix well to remove any lumps.

Divide the mixture in two and press it into the two round tins. Prick it well and sprinkle with granulated sugar.

Put the tins in the oven and bake until the shortbread is golden brown, about three-quarters of an hour. Take the tins out of the oven and cut into pieces while the shortbread is still warm.

Chapter Fourteen
What Do You Know?

Quick Quiz: for this quiz you need a watch with a second hand, to time the players accurately. The aim is to give as many words as possible beginning with a given letter in a minute (or two minutes or thirty seconds, or whatever is decided). The players take turns. The leader announces the chosen letter, saying, for instance 'T – go!' The player then rattles off as many words as he can before his time is up. The winner is the person who manages to say the largest number of words.

Initials: what do the following initials stand for?

1. RN	18. CWS	34. STD	50. eg
2. RAF	19. ER	35. LCM	51. NUT
3. RNVR	20. HCF	36. YMCA	52. OK
4. AWOL	21. WRVS	37. TGWU	53. BA
5. OM	22. GI	38. SS	54. BR
6. PTO	23. BBC	39. FBI	55. NB
7. RASC	24. sae	40. DD	56. AA
8. HMS	25. COD	41. BC	57. RSPCA
9. JP	26. HQ	42. FRUTB	58. SOS
10. ie	27. GCE	43. ITA	59. CID
11. TUC	28. QC	44. UK	60. E & OE
12. HRH	29. AB	45. USA	61. MOH
13. GPO	30. OHMS	46. c/o	62. LBW
14. AD	31. VC	47. RIP	63. DSO
15. RAC	32. USSR	48. C of E	64. VIP
16. pm	33. C-in-C	49. IOU	65. FHB
17. WHO			

First Names: the question gives the surnames of famous people in fact or fiction, and the players give the first name.

1. Dickens	18. Galilei	35. Newton
2. da Gama	19. Franklin	36. da Vinci
3. Nelson	20. Bunny	37. Shakespeare
4. Reynolds	21. Churchill	38. Cromwell
5. Kipling	22. Bonaparte	39. Fonteyn
6. Beethoven	23. Columbus	40. Sawyer
7. Constable	24. Picasso	41. Puddleduck
8. Austen	25. Bach	42. Twist
9. Edison	26. Cook	43. Britten
10. Hillary	27. Wren	44. Wesley
11. Polo	28. Drake	45. Raleigh
12. Luther	29. Charlton	46. Caxton
13. Curie	30. Nightingale	47. Washington
14. Lincoln	31. Hood	48. Whittington
15. Pasteur	32. Chaucer	49. Wordsworth
16. Best	33. McCartney	50. van Gogh
17. Pan	34. Whiskers	51. March

Mr, Mrs, and Baby Who? the question master gives the name of the male animal, and the players tell the names of the female, the young, and the general family name.

1. Ram	5. Boar	9. Drake
2. Stag	6. Bull	10. Cock
3. Lion	7. Stallion	11. Gander
4. Dog	8. Billy-goat	12. Cob

How Many a Side? How many players are there on each team in the following games?

1. Soccer	5. Tennis	9. Golf
2. Netball	6. Squash	10. Rugby Union; League
3. Rounders	7. Baseball	11. Polo
4. Hockey	8. Cricket	12. Lacrosse

Where Do They Play It? Where did the following sports originate?

1. Cricket
2. Basketball
3. Lacrosse
4. Baseball
5. Curling
6. Squash
7. Golf
8. Polo
9. Bull-fighting
10. Ice Hockey

Famous Names: for what are these people famous?

1. Sir Francis Drake
2. Sir Francis Chichester
3. Alcock and Brown
4. Yehudi Menuhin
5. Henry Moore
6. Colin Cowdrey
7. Marie Curie
8. Julie Andrews
9. Sir Christopher Wren
10. Sir Laurence Olivier
11. John Lennon
12. Bobby Charlton
13. Sherpa Tensing
14. William Gladstone
15. Alexander Fleming
16. Florence Nightingale
17. Thomas Jefferson
18. Martin Luther King
19. Alexander Graham Bell
20. John Keats

What is it?

1. a cab
2. a sundial
3. a steeple-jack
4. a steeplechase
5. a penny-farthing
6. a bun penny
7. a robot
8. a jumble sale
9. a 'cello
10. a marquis
11. a marquee
12. a vacuum
13. a county
14. mistletoe
15. a bolster
16. a harp
17. a harpoon
18. an aviary
19. an apiary
20. jodhpurs
21. a samovar
22. garlic
23. a puff ball
24. a dumpling
25. a parachute
26. a dumb-bell
27. a ferry
28. a toll-gate
29. a casserole
30. a manger
31. a mangel-wurzel
32. a flan

33. a flat iron
34. a manuscript
35. a paediatrician
36. a basement
37. an escalator
38. a courier
39. a gymnasium
40. pieces of eight

Who Eats What? If you were offered these foods in their native land, where would you be? And what would you expect to find on your plate?

1. frogs' legs
2. paella
3. curry
4. bortsch
5. sauerkraut
6. goulash
7. bird's nest soup
8. hamburger
9. cous-cous
10. smorgasbord
11. haggis
12. fondue
13. dolmas
14. tamale
15. ravioli
16. piperade
17. Wiener schnitzel
18. shish-kebab
19. pizza
20. pumpkin pie
21. simnel cake

Who Wears It? In what countries did the following clothes originate? And what are they like?

1. kimono
2. dirndl
3. kilt
4. sari
5. fez
6. jodhpurs
7. pyjamas
8. tuxedo
9. chaps
10. poncho
11. dhoti
12. kaftan
13. bowler
14. moccasin
15. beret
16. mantilla
17. topee
18. chomsan
19. toga
20. turban
21. parka
22. sombrero
23. yashmak
24. sabots

Place Associations: the following places are associated with certain foods or other products. Do you know what they are?

1. Gloucester
2. Montelimar
3. Bath
4. Melton Mowbray
5. Nottingham
6. Cheddar
7. Chelsea
8. Jerusalem
9. Waterford
10. Jaffa
11. Seville
12. Worcester
13. Dundee
14. York
15. Edinburgh
16. Eccles
17. Frankfurt
18. Dresden

World Tour: if you were on a world tour, to which country would you go to see:

1. The Vatican
2. The Pyramids
3. A koala bear
4. Stonehenge
5. The Eiffel Tower
6. The Statue of the Little Mermaid
7. Tower Bridge
8. The Mona Lisa
9. A beaver
10. Sidney Bridge
11. Mount Fujiyama
12. The Grand Canyon
13. An Anteater
14. The Acropolis
15. The Taj Mahal
16. The Statue of Liberty
17. Covent Garden
18. The Alps
19. The Colosseum
20. The Blue Danube
21. The Costa Brava
22. The Blarney Stone
23. The Nile
24. The Great Wall
25. A yak

Pairs: the following pairs of words sound the same, and may even be spelt the same, but have different meanings. Can you give both meanings?

1. grill – grille
2. marble – marble
3. knave – nave
4. sage – sage
5. boy – buoy
6. cairn – cairn
7. cricket – cricket
8. duck – duck
9. kernel – colonel
10. flower – flour

Nicknames: the following are 'nicknames' for various countries or cities; how many of them can you identify?

1. The Emerald Isle
2. The Garden of England
3. The Land of the Midnight Sun
4. The Land of the Rising Sun
5. The Land of Milk and Honey
6. The Barbary Coast
7. The Bride of the Sea
8. The Eternal City
9. The Fatherland
10. The Dark Continent
11. The Holy City
12. The Spice Islands
13. The Athens of the North
14. The Windy City
15. The Antipodes

Who Said? Here are some sayings from history or fiction. Who said them?

1. No more twist.
2. A horse! a horse! my kingdom for a horse!
3. I came, I saw, I conquered.
4. If at first you don't succeed, try, try again.
5. Eureka!
6. What big eyes you have!
7. To be or not to be, that is the question.
8. Kiss me, Hardy.
9. God bless us every one!
10. You can fool all the people some of the time, and some of the people all the time, but you cannot fool all the people all of the time.
11. Curiouser and curiouser!
12. Annual income twenty pounds, annual expenditure nineteen nineteen six, result happiness. Annual income twenty pounds, annual expenditure twenty pounds ought and six, result misery.
13. Till death do us part.
14. Elementary, my dear Watson.
15. When I am dead and opened, you shall find 'Calais' lying in my heart.

16. Dear Pig, are you willing to sell for one shilling your ring?
17. Abandon hope, all ye who enter here!
18. Nevermore.
19. Long live our noble King!
20. Bred en bawn in a brier-patch!
21. When shall we three meet again . . .
22. Open Sesame!
23. Give us the tools and we will finish the job.
24. For auld lang syne.
25. A place for everything and everything in its place.
26. Dr Livingstone, I presume?
27. Time for a little something.
28. We are not amused.
29. Theirs not to reason why
    Theirs but to do and die.

Highway Code Quiz: have a copy of The Highway Code in the car and ask each other questions from it. Here are some suggestions.

Rules of the Road

1. What's the rule about crossing the road?
2. Do you have the right to cross the road on a zebra crossing whenever you wish?
3. What is the order of the lights on a set of traffic lights?
4. What do the different traffic light colours mean?
   a. Red b. Red and Amber c. Green d. Amber
5. What is the rule about getting on and off a bus?
6. When should you wear a safety helmet?
7. Which side of the road do you drive on in Britain?
8. Which side of the road do you drive on in France?
9. What does a double white line down the middle of the road mean?
10. There are six places where you should never overtake

when you are at them or coming towards them. What do you think they are?

11. When should you *not* sound your horn?
12. What must you have on your bicycle when you are driving at night?
13. Which side of the road should you walk on when there is no footpath?
14. What should you wear or carry when you are walking along a road at night?
15. What is the traffic sign for keep left?
16. What is the sign for no cycling or moped riding?
17. What is the sign for no entry?

General knowledge

1. Who were the six wives of Henry VIII?
2. What are the eight Royal houses of England since 1066?
3. What were the seven wonders of the Ancient World?
4. Can you name 20 counties in England?
5. Can you name 20 countries in Europe and their capital cities?
6. Can you name 20 States of America?
7. Can you name the seven continents?
8. Can you describe and name the three flags which make up the Union Jack?
9. What are the five senses?
10. What is the Decalogue?
11. What are the four elements of the Ancient World?
12. How long is a decade?
13. How long is a millennium?
14. To what does this poem refer?
    Snowy, Flowy, Blowy,
    Showery, Flowery, Bowery,
    Hoppy, Croppy, Droppy,
    Breezy, Sneezy, Freezy.
15. Name all the prime numbers (or numbers which cannot be divided by any other number) up to 100.

Geography Quiz:

1. Where is the Panama Canal?
2. What is an archipelago?
3. Where is Cape Horn?
4. What is Quebec?
5. Where is the Kalahari Desert?
6. Where do gorillas come from?
7. What is an isthmus?
8. Where are the Niagara Falls?
9. Where is the Rhine?
10. What is a wallaby and where does it live?

History Quiz:

1. What happened on Christmas Day, 1066?
2. Who was Ghandi?
3. Who came to Britain in 55 BC?
4. What was a Pharaoh?
5. What was a Boer?
6. What happened in France in 1789?
7. What was a Peeler and why was he called this?
8. In what years did the First and Second World Wars start and end?
9. Who was Bonnie Prince Charlie?
10. Who were the Princes in the Tower?

Who Wrote? . . .

1. *Black Beauty*
2. *Beau Geste*
3. *On the Origin of Species*
4. *War and Peace*
5. *The Children of the New Forest*
6. *Little Lord Fauntleroy*
7. *Coral Island*
8. *Oliver Twist*
9. *The Tale of the Pie and the Patty Pan*
10. *Northanger Abbey*

11. *The Weirdstone of Brisingham*
12. *Finn Family Moomintroll*
13. *Cranford*
14. *For Whom the Bell Tolls*
15. *Moonfleet*
16. *King Solomon's Mines*
17. *Stig of the Dump*
18. *Wuthering Heights*
19. *Hercule Poirot's Christmas*
20. *Little Grey Rabbit's Christmas*
21. *Peter Duck*
22. *Tom Sawyer*
23. *The Secret Seven*
24. *Ivanhoe*
25. *Babar*
26. *Orlando the Marmalade Cat*
27. *Just William*
28. *The Borrowers*
29. *The Wind in the Willows*
30. *The Jungle Book*
31. *The Story of the Little Tin Soldier*
32. *The Silver Sword*
33. *The Lion, the Witch and the Wardrobe*
34. *The Odyssey*
35. *A Swarm in May*
36. *Peter Pan*
37. *The Sign of Four*
38. *The House at Pooh Corner*
39. *Smith*
40. *Tom's Midnight Garden*
41. *The Midnight Folk*
42. *The Cuckoo Clock*
43. *Anne of Green Gables*
44. *A Hundred and One Dalmatians*
45. *The Railway Children*
46. *Kidnapped*
47. *The Kon-tiki Expedition*

48. *The Little House in the Big Wood*
49. *Tarzan of the Apes*
50. *Ring of Bright Water*

Literary Quiz:

1. Who asked for more?
2. What is Poohsticks?
3. What is a Pollyanna and why?
4. Who saved Red Riding Hood from a frightful death?
5. Who eloped with the Dish?
6. Who learnt reeling and writhing and fainting in coils?
7. Who went about ticking?
8. Who owing to his disobedience had no toes?
9. Who suffered from 'satiable curtiosity'?
10. In E. Nesbit's book *Five Children and It*, what is It?
11. Why did Amy March put a clothes-peg on her nose?
12. Who made whom into a roly-poly pudding?
13. Who loved 'just messing about in boats'?
14. Who was the Owl of the Remove?
15. What was the Owl Service?
16. What *is* it that Tiggers like?
17. What was the name of the Hobbit's house?
18. Who sang 'Fifteen men on a dead man's chest'?
19. What were the names of the Amazon pirates?
20. Who had a fox, a crow and a squirrel as pets?

Myth and Legend:

1. Whose look turned people to stone?
2. Whose touch turned everything to gold?
3. Whose song lured sailors to destruction?
4. Whose spell turned men to swine?
5. Whose face 'launched a thousand ships'?
6. Who fell in love with his own reflection?
7. Where did the Minotaur live and what was it?
8. Who sprang fully-armed from her father's brow?
9. Who was killed when he flew too near the sun?
10. Who was brought up by a centaur?

Answers to Chapter Four
Think of a Number

Think of a Number (page 30)
What you have done here if you look carefully is to multiply by 10 and add 3.

Number Puzzle and Trick Questions (page 32)
1. *Cannibals and Missionaries*
    1. Cannibal and Missionary cross. M rows back.
    2. C and C cross. C rows back.
    3. M and M cross. M and C row back.
    4. M and M cross. C rows back.
    5. C and C cross. C. rows back.
    6. Cannibal and Cannibal cross.

2. None. The ship will rise on the tide and the ladder with it.
3. Neither. They both weigh a ton.
4. G. This is a straight alphabet in sequence series.
   T. Miss one, miss two, miss three, etc.
   16. Each number is double the one before.

Riddles and Trick Questions (page 36)
1. An umbrella.
2. A newspaper (for red is spelt read here).
3. A rubbish cart.
4. A centipede with a wooden leg.
5. I–T.
6. A candle.
7. One is made of wood and the other is Maid of Orleans.

8. One is an animal and the other is to wash your face in.
9. If you don't know, I shan't send *you* to post my letters!
10. To get to the other side, or for some foul reason or other.
11. In the dark.
12. A person was sitting on a three-legged stool when in came a dog.
13. Well, you asked for it!
14. Hailing taxis.
15. Half a worm.

Conundrums (page 37)

1. Bacon.
2. B (ee).
3. T (ea).
4. Ash.
5. Beauty.
6. When it is a-jar.
7. Bleeding heart.
8. Pau-city.
9. Because he reigns (rains).
10. Vege-table.

Answers to Chapter Fourteen
Did You Know?

Initials

1. Royal Navy.
2. Royal Air Force.
3. Royal Naval Volunteer Reserve.
4. Absent Without Leave.
5. Order of Merit.
6. Please turn over.
7. Royal Army Service Corps.
8. Her Majesty's Ship.
9. Justice of the Peace.
10. *id est*, that is.
11. Trades Union Congress.
12. His/Her Royal Highness.
13. General Post Office.
14. *Anno Domini*, in the year of Our Lord.
15. Royal Automobile Club.
16. *post meridiem*, after noon.
17. World Health Organization.
18. Co-operative Wholesale Society.
19. Elizabeth Regina.
20. Highest common factor.
21. Women's Royal Voluntary Service.
22. General Issue (US Army Private).
23. British Broadcasting Corporation.
24. Stamped addressed envelope.
25. Cash on delivery.
26. Headquarters.
27. General Certificate of Education.
28. Queen's Counsel.
29. Able-bodied seaman.
30. On Her Majesty's Service.
31. Victoria Cross.
32. Union of Soviet Socialist Republics.
33. Commander-in-Chief.
34. Subscriber Trunk Dialling.
35. Lowest common multiple.
36. Young Men's Christian Association.

37. Transport and General Workers' Union.
38. Steamship.
39. Federal Bureau of Investigation.
40. Doctor of Divinity.
41. Before Christ.
42. Full right up to busting.
43. Independent Television Authority.
44. United Kingdom.
45. United States of America.
46. Care of.
47. *Requiescat in pace,* may he/she rest in peace.
48. Church of England.
49. I owe you.
50. *exempli gratia,* for example.
51. National Union of Teachers.
52. Oll Korrect (misspelling of 'All Correct').
53. Bachelor of Arts.
54. British Rail.
55. *Nota bene,* note well.
56. Automobile Association, Architectural Association.
57. Royal Society for the Prevention of Cruelty to Animals.
58. Save our Souls (distress signal).
59. Criminal Investigation Department.
60. Errors and Omissions Excepted.
61. Medical Officer of Health.
62. Leg Before Wicket (cricket).
63. Distinguished Service Order (Medal).
64. Very Important Person.
65. Family Hold Back.

First Names:

1. Charles
2. Vasco
3. Horatio
4. Joshua
5. Rudyard
6. Ludwig
7. John
8. Jane
9. Thomas
10. Edmund
11. Marco
12. Martin
13. Marie/Pierre
14. Abraham
15. Louis
16. George

17. Peter
18. Galileo
19. Benjamin
20. Benjamin
21. Winston
22. Napoleon
23. Christopher
24. Pablo
25. Johann Sebastian
26. James
27. Christopher
28. Francis
29. Bobby
30. Florence
31. Robin/Thomas
32. Geoffrey
33. Paul
34. Samuel
35. Isaac
36. Leonardo
37. William
38. Oliver/Thomas
39. Margot
40. Tom
41. Jemima
42. Oliver
43. Benjamin
44. John
45. Walter
46. William
47. George
48. Dick
49. William
50. Vincent
51. Meg, Jo, Beth, Amy

Mr, Mrs, and Baby Who:

1. Ewe, lamb, sheep.
2. Hind/doe, fawn, deer.
3. Lioness, cub, lion.
4. Bitch, puppy, dog.
5. Sow, piglet, pig.
6. Cow, calf, cattle.
7. Mare, foal, horse.
8. Nanny-goat, kid, goat.
9. Duck, duckling, duck.
10. Hen, chick, chicken.
11. Goose, gosling, goose.
12. Pen, cygnet, swan.

How Many a Side?

1. 11
2. 7
3. 9
4. 11
5. 1 or 2
6. 1 or 2
7. 9
8. 11
9. 1 or 2
10. 15 (U); 13 (L)
11. 4
12. 12 (10 in US or Canada)

Where Do They Play It?

1. England
2. USA
3. Canada
4. USA
5. Scotland
6. England
7. Scotland
8. Persia, Tibet, Assam, Japan
9. Spain
10. Canada

Famous Names:

1. Admiral against the Armada, the first ship's captain to circumnavigate the world, 1577–80.
2. The first person to circumnavigate the world single-handed, 1966–7.
3. First to fly the Atlantic, 1919.
4. Violinist.
5. Sculptor and painter.
6. Cricketer.
7. Discoverer, with her husband Pierre, of radium.
8. Actress and singer.
9. Architect, especially famous for having built St Paul's Cathedral.
10. Actor.
11. Pop music writer and singer, one of the Beatles.
12. Footballer.
13. With Sir Edmund Hillary, the first to reach the summit of Mount Everest, 1953.
14. Politician, Prime Minister of Britain under Queen Victoria.
15. Discoverer of penicillin.
16. Organized the nursing in the Crimean War, formed an institute for the training of nurses, helped found the Red Cross.
17. Third President of USA, drafted the American Declaration of Independence.
18. Negro Civil Rights leader in USA.
19. Inventor of the telephone.
20. Poet.

What is it?

1. A public carriage, with 2 or 4 wheels, horse-drawn, to seat 2 or 4 people; the word is now used for a taxi; the covered part of a locomotive which shelters the engine driver.
2. Shows the time of day by means of the shadow of a marker cast by the sun upon a surface marked with a diagram showing the hours.
3. A man who climbs steeples or tall chimneys to repair them.
4. A horse-race across country or on a made course with artificial fences, water-jumps and other obstacles. Formerly a race having a church steeple in view as goal, in which all intervening obstacles had to be cleared.
5. An old-fashioned high bicycle, having a large wheel in front and a small one behind.
6. A penny with the head of the young Queen Victoria on it, showing her hair in a 'bun' (that is, hair coiled up in the shape of a bun).
7. A machine made to do something instead of a living person; a living being that acts automatically.
8. A sale, usually for charity, of wildly miscellaneous items, from home-made cakes to old boots.
9. Short for violon-cello, a large four-stringed instrument of the violin family.
10. In England, a degree of peerage between earl and duke.
11. A large tent, like one used for a wedding or garden fête.
12. A space empty of air, or (left) unoccupied or unfilled by its usual contents.
13. One of the territorial divisions of the United Kingdom.
14. A parasitic plant which grows in a ball-shape on trees. It has a whitish berry and green leaves. Mistletoe is hung up at Christmas-time and people meeting under it are supposed to exchange kisses.

15. A long stuffed pillow or cushion.
16. A musical instrument with a triangular framework with strings, which are plucked with the fingers, stretched across it.
17. A barbed spear with a long line attached to it, used for capturing whales and large fish. It is hurled by hand or shot from a gun, and can then be hauled back.
18. A large cage, house or enclosure in which birds are kept.
19. A place where bees are kept.
20. Riding breeches.
21. A Russian tea-urn.
22. A plant with a bulbous root which has a very strong smell and taste; the root is used in cooking or salads.
23. A fungus which has a ball-like shape. It lets out spores in a puff of white powder when broken.
24. A mass of dough boiled in soups or stews or boiled or baked with fruit inside as a pudding.
25. An apparatus like a huge umbrella, used for descending safely from an aeroplane in flight.
26. A short bar weighted at each end with a round knob, swung in pairs for exercise.
27. A place where boats cross back and forth to carry passengers and goods.
28. A barrier across a road where a tax (or toll) is collected to pay for the use of the road.
29. A kind of stew pan; or the dish cooked in one, usually a sort of stew with meat and vegetables.
30. A trough or box in a stable or cowshed from which horses or cattle eat.
31. A sort of beet, used as food for cattle.
32. An open tart with fruit, etc, in it.
33. An old-fashioned iron which had to be heated by the fire.
34. A book or document written by hand, though often

now a typed document is called a manuscript.

35. A doctor specializing in the treatment of children.
36. The lowest storey of a building, partly or completely underground.
37. A moving staircase.
38. A running messenger; someone who makes all the arrangements for a journey.
39. A building where athletes train or where physical education is given.
40. The old Spanish dollar, marked with the 8 because it was worth 8 *reals.*

Who Eats What?

1. France or Italy. Served in a sauce – said to taste like chicken.
2. Spain. A dish of rice with bits of seafood, chicken, peppers, etc, cooked with it.
3. India, Pakistan, most of the Far East. Meat or vegetables cooked with pungent spices, such as chilli, turmeric, ginger, etc.
4. Russia. Beetroot soup, very rich and served with sour cream on top.
5. Germany and Austria. Cabbage pickled in vinegar.
6. Hungary. A meat stew with paprika.
7. China. A broth containing the edible nest of a bird found in the China Sea.
8. USA. A minced beef patty, served in a sliced round bun, usually with onions.
9. North Africa. Coarse flour (like semolina) cooked by steaming over broth or meat.
10. Scandinavia. Open sandwiches made with fish, meat, salad, etc.
11. Scotland. The heart, lungs and liver of a sheep, minced with suet and oatmeal and onions and boiled in a sheep's stomach.
12. Switzerland, France. A savoury cheese sauce,

served in a bowl into which people dip bits of bread or meat.

13. Turkey, Near East. Minced meat cooked in vine or cabbage leaves.
14. Mexico. Crushed Indian corn, flavoured with meat, red pepper, etc, and baked.
15. Italy. Small squares of pasta, each piece being two squares stuck together with meat in the middle.
16. France. Green peppers, tomatoes, onion, garlic and herbs cooked to a pulp and mixed with scrambled egg.
17. Austria. Veal fillet cut very thin and cooked in bread-crumbs. 'Wiener' means 'of Vienna'.
18. Turkey, Near East. Small chunks of meat and vegetables alternated on a skewer and grilled.
19. Italy. A flat circle of bread dough, covered with tomato purée, cheese, olives, anchovies and herbs.
20. USA. A pastry shell filled with a custard made of sieved pumpkin, spices, milk and eggs.
21. England. A traditional cake originally baked for Mothering Sunday, now usually at Easter. A rich fruit cake with layers of almond paste in it, decorated with balls of almond paste.

Who Wears It?

1. Japan. A wrap-around robe with flowing sleeves.
2. Austria. A full-skirted pinafore dress worn with an apron.
3. Scotland. A pleated skirt, worn by men.
4. India. Length of cloth wrapped round the body to make a dress.
5. Morocco. A brimless hat.
6. India. Riding breeches cut very full over the hips, but tightly fitting from knee to ankle. Jodhpur is a town in north-west India.
7. Turkey. Loose cotton suit.

8. USA. Evening jacket.
9. USA. Leather over-trousers to protect the legs when riding.
10. Mexico. A circular cape with no fastening, instead a hole for the head.
11. India. Cloth wrapped round the body to form trousers.
12. Turkey, Persia. A long robe.
13. England. A hard round hat, usually black.
14. Canada. Soft Red Indian shoe.
15. France. A flat pull-on hat.
16. Spain. A lace head-dress.
17. British India. A large, hard hat worn to protect the wearer from the sun.
18. China. Straight dress, slit at the sides.
19. Ancient Rome. A long robe.
20. Moslem countries. Head-dress made by winding a cloth around the head.
21. Canada. Jacket like an anorak.
22. Mexico. Large-brimmed hat.
23. Moslem countries. A veil worn to hide the face.
24. Holland, France. Wooden shoes.

Place Associations:

1. Cheese	7. Buns	13. Cake
2. Sweet, nougat	8. Artichokes	14. Ham
3. Buns, bathchairs	9. Glass	15. Rock
4. Pork pies	10. Oranges	16. Cakes
5. Lace	11. Oranges	17. Sausages
6. Cheese	12. Sauce	18. China

World Tour:

1. Italy	6. Denmark	11. Japan
2. Egypt	7. England	12. USA
3. Australia	8. France	13. South America
4. England	9. Canada	14. Greece
5. France	10. Australia	15. India

16. USA
17. England
18. Switzerland, Austria, Germany, France, Italy
19. Italy
20. Austria/ Hungary
21. Spain
22. Ireland
23. Egypt
24. China
25. Tibet

Pairs:

1. a. The grid for cooking food under heat; the meat or fish cooked on one.
   b. A grating.
2. a. Limestone which can be highly polished and is used in sculpture and buildings.
   b. A small ball (originally made of marble) now made of china or glass, used in children's games.
3. a. Originally a boy, but now mainly meaning a rogue; the Jack in a pack of cards.
   b. The main part of a church from the inner door to the choir or chancel.
4. a. An aromatic herb with silvery grey leaves.
   b. A wise man.
5. a. A male child.
   b. A floating object fastened in a particular place to point out the position of things underwater, or the course for ships.
6. a. A pile of rough stones, as a landmark, boundary mark, or memorial.
   b. The smallest breed of British terrier.
7. a. An open-air game played with bats, a ball and wickets by two sides of 11 players each.
   b. An insect.
8. a. A web-footed swimming bird.
   b. A strong cloth used for small sails and men's (especially sailors') clothing.
9. a. A seed, especially one within any fruit or nut.
   b. A senior officer in the Army.
10. a. A blossom, bloom.
    b. Finely ground meal of, usually, wheat.

Nicknames:

1. Ireland
2. Kent
3. Norway, Lapland
4. Japan
5. The Biblical land of Canaan
6. North Africa
7. Venice
8. Rome
9. Germany
10. Africa
11. Jerusalem
12. Moluccas, East Indies
13. Edinburgh
14. Chicago
15. Australia and New Zealand

Who Said?

1. The mice in *The Tailor of Gloucester* by Beatrix Potter.
2. Richard III, in Shakespeare's *King Richard III.*
3. Julius Caesar, according to Plutarch.
4. W. E. Hickson in poem 'Try and try again'.
5. Archimedes.
6. Little Red Riding Hood.
7. Hamlet, in *Hamlet* by William Shakespeare.
8. It is attributed to Nelson dying at Trafalgar.
9. Tiny Tim in Charles Dickens' *A Christmas Carol.*
10. Abraham Lincoln.
11. Alice in *Alice in Wonderland* by Lewis Carroll.
12. Mr Micawber, in *David Copperfield* by Dickens.
13. Solemnization of Marriage, Book of Common Prayer.
14. It is always supposed, Sherlock Holmes in one of Conan Coyle's stories, but he never actually said these exact words.
15. Mary Tudor.
16. *The Owl and the Pussy Cat* by Edward Lear.
17. Dante, in the *Divine Comedy, Inferno.*
18. The raven in Edgar Allen Poe's poem *The Raven.*
19. Henry Carey (1693–1743), song.
20. Brer Rabbit in Joel Chandler Harris' *Uncle Remus.*
21. The first Witch in Shakespeare's *Macbeth.*
22. Ali Baba, in *The Arabian Nights.*

23. Winston Churchill, 1941, in a radio broadcast to President Roosevelt.
24. Robert Burns, in the song, *Auld Lang Syne.*
25. Samuel Smiles in *Thrift.*
26. Sir Henry Stanley.
27. Pooh, in A. A. Milne's *Winnie-the-Pooh.*
28. Queen Victoria.
29. Tennyson's *The Charge of the Light Brigade.*

Rules of the Road

1. Stop at the kerb; look right, look left, look right again; when the road is clear, cross; go quickly, but do not run.
2. No. Traffic must give way when you are *on* the crossing, but you must give cars plenty of time to stop before you step onto the crossing.
3. Red, Red+Amber, Green, Amber, Red.
4. Red = stop behind stop line on the road.
   Red+Amber = stop until green light shows.
   Green = go on if the way is clear.
   Amber = stop at the stop line unless you have already crossed it.
5. Do not get on or off a bus unless it is standing at a bus stop.
6. When you are riding a motor cycle, scooter or moped.
7. Left.
8. Right.
9. A double white line down the middle of the road means that you must not cross it unless you are turning to the right off the road.
10. You should never overtake at or when you are coming towards:

a pedestrian crossing	a hump-back bridge
a road junction	the brow of a hill
a corner or bend	a level crossing.

Can you say why you should not overtake at each of these places?

11. When your vehicle is stopped on the road; in a built-up area between 11.30 PM and 7 AM.
12. You must have front and rear lights and a red reflector at the back. All of them must be working.
13. Walk on the right-hand side of the road, facing the oncoming traffic.
14. Wear or carry something white, or light coloured, or something which reflects light.
15. A white arrow on a blue ground pointing downwards to the left.
16. A bicycle in a red circle. (All traffic signals in a red frame give an instruction or warning.)
17. A thick white horizontal line on a red circular background.

General Knowledge

1. Katharine of Aragon, Anne Boleyn, Jane Seymour, Anne of Cleves, Catherine Howard, Katharine Parr.
2. A clue sentence: 'No plan like yours to study history wisely'. Norman, Plantagenet, Lancaster, York, Tudor, Stuart, Hanover, Windsor.
3. The Pyramids of Egypt; the Hanging Gardens of Babylon; the Tomb of Mausolus, King of Caria; the Temple of Diana of Ephesus; the Colossus at Rhodes; the gold and ivory statue of Jupiter Olympus; the Pharos at Alexandria (a lighthouse).
4. Northumberland, Cumberland, Durham, Westmorland, Yorkshire, Lancashire, Cheshire, Derbyshire, Lincolnshire, Staffordshire, Shropshire, Herefordshire, Warwickshire, Leicestershire, Rutland, Huntingdonshire, Norfolk, Suffolk, Essex, Bedfordshire, Hertfordshire, Oxfordshire, Cambridgeshire, Gloucestershire, Wiltshire, Hampshire, Surrey, Sussex, Kent, Dorset, Devonshire, Somerset, Cornwall.

5. Great Britain, London; France, Paris; Norway, Oslo; Sweden, Stockholm; Denmark, Copenhagen; Finland, Helsinki; USSR, Moscow; West Germany, Bonn; Belgium, Brussels; Netherlands, The Hague; Austria, Vienna; Switzerland, Berne; Spain, Madrid; Portugal, Lisbon; Eire, Dublin; Luxembourg, Luxembourg; Italy, Rome; Poland, Warsaw; Czechoslovakia, Prague; Hungary, Budapest; Romania, Bucharest; Yugoslavia, Belgrade; Albania, Tirana; Greece, Athens; Monte Carlo, Monte Carlo.
6. Indiana, Ohio, Pennsylvania, Vermont, New Hampshire, Maine, Massachusetts, Connecticut, New York, New Jersey, Delaware, Washington, Virginia, West Virginia, Kentucky, Illinois, Kansas, Florida, Texas, New Mexico, California, Arizona, Colorado, Minnesota, Missouri, Mississippi, Maryland, Nevada, North Carolina, South Carolina, Wyoming, Utah, Louisiana, Arkansas, Rhode Island, Georgia, Oklahoma, Idaho, Oregon, Montana, Iowa, Tennessee, Alabama, Alaska, Hawaii.
7. Europe, Asia, North America, South America, Africa, Australia, Antarctica.
8. Red cross (+) on white ground, St George; White cross (×) on blue ground, St Andrew; red cross (×) on white ground, St Patrick.
9. Sight, hearing, touch, smell, taste.
10. The Ten Commandments.
11. Earth, air, fire and water.
12. Ten years.
13. A thousand years.
14. The twelve months of the year.
15. 1, 3, 5, 7, 11, 13, 17, 19, 23, 29, 31, 37, 41, 43, 47, 53, 59, 61, 67, 71, 73, 79, 83, 89, 91, 97.

Geography Quiz:

1. At Panama, on the thinnest piece of land between North and South America.
2. A group of islands.
3. At the southern tip of South America.
4. A province and city in Eastern Canada.
5. Southern Africa.
6. West Equatorial Africa.
7. A narrow neck of land, enclosed on each side by water, and connecting two larger bodies of land.
8. On the border between Canada and the USA.
9. Germany.
10. A small kangaroo-like animal. Australia.

History Quiz

1. William the Conqueror was crowned King of England.
2. An Indian leader, who did much to further independence in India.
3. Julius Caesar.
4. A ruler in Ancient Egypt.
5. A Dutch colonist in South Africa.
6. The beginning of the French Revolution.
7. A policeman. Originally a nickname for the Irish Constabulary, founded 1812–18 by Mr (later Sir) Robert Peel.
8. 1914–18; 1939–45.
9. Charles Edward Stuart, the Young Pretender, grandson of James II.
10. Edward V and Richard, Duke of York, sons of Edward IV.

Who Wrote ? . . .

1. Anna Sewell
2. P. C. Wren
3. Charles Darwin
4. Leo Tolstoy
5. Captain Marryat
6. Frances Hodgson Burnett
7. R. D. Ballantyne
8. Charles Dickens
9. Beatrix Potter
10. Jane Austen
11. Alan Garner
12. Tove Jansen
13. Mrs Gaskell
14. Ernest Hemingway
15. Meade Faulkner
16. Rider Haggard
17. Clive King
18. Emily Brontë
19. Agatha Christie
20. Alison Uttley
21. Arthur Ransome
22. Mark Twain
23. Enid Blyton
24. Sir Walter Scott
25. Louis Brunhof
26. Kathleen Hale
27. Richmal Crompton
28. Cicely Norton
29. Kenneth Grahame
30. Rudyard Kipling
31. Hans Anderson
32. Ian Seraillier
33. C. S. Lewis
34. Homer
35. William Mayne
36. J. M. Barrie
37. Arthur Conan Doyle
38. A. A. Milne
39. Leon Garfield
40. Philippa Pearce
41. John Masefield
42. Mrs Molesworth
43. L. M. Montgomery
44. Dodie Smith
45. E. Nesbit
46. R. L. Stevenson
47. Thor Heyerdahl
48. Laura Ingalls Wilder
49. E. R. Burroughs
50. Gavin Maxwell

Literary Quiz

1. Oliver Twist.
2. A game invented by Pooh in which people standing on a bridge each drop a stick into the water on the upstream side and then run to the other side to see whose stick appears first.
3. A person who always looks on the bright side; from *Pollyana* by Eleanor Porter, about a little girl who did just that.

4. A woodcutter.
5. The Spoon.
6. The Mock Turtle in *Alice in Wonderland.*
7. The crocodile in *Peter Pan*, who had swallowed an alarm clock.
8. The Pobble in a poem by Edward Lear.
9. 'The Elephant's Child' in the *Just So Stories* by Rudyard Kipling.
10. The Psammead, a magic creature who could grant wishes.
11. To try and stop it turning up. She is one of Louisa May Alcott's *Little Women.*
12. Henrietta Maria Whiskers made Tom Kitten into a pudding in Beatrix Potter's story *The Roly-Poly Pudding.*
13. Ratty in *The Wind in the Willows* by Kenneth Grahame.
14. Billy Bunter.
15. A dinner service, in the book of that name by Alan Garner.
16. Cod liver oil and Malt.
17. Bag-end.
18. The Pirates in *Treasure Island* by R. L. Stevenson.
19. Nancy and Peggy Blackett in *Swallows and Amazons* by Arthur Ransome.
20. Dickon in *The Secret Garden* by Frances Hodgson Burnett.

Myth and Legend

1. The Gorgon, Medusa.
2. Midas.
3. The Sirens.
4. Circe.
5. Helen of Troy.
6. Narcissus.

7. A bull-headed monster in the labyrinth in Knossos, Crete.
8. Athene.
9. Icarus.
10. Jason.

Colour Books and Fiction

COLOUR BOOKS

Great new titles for boys and girls from eight to twelve. Fascinating full-colour pictures on every page. Intriguing, authentic easy-to-read facts.

DINOSAURS Jane Werner Watson
SECRETS OF THE PAST Eva Knox Evans
SCIENCE AND US Bertha Morris Parker
INSIDE THE EARTH
Rose Wyler and Gerald Ames
EXPLORING OTHER WORLDS
Rose Wyler and Gerald Ames
STORMS Paul E. Lehr
SNAKES AND OTHER REPTILES
George S. Fichter
AIRBORNE ANIMALS George S. Fichter

25p each Fit your pocket – Suit your purse

FICTION

For younger readers

ALBERT AND HENRY
Alison Jezard 20p
ALBERT IN SCOTLAND
Alison Jezard 20p